IMMIGRATION REFORM

Pathway to Bi-Partisan Legislation that will Rectify this Decades-Long Political Debacle

Joe M. Sifuentez

CONTENTS

ABOUT THE AUTHOR

Joe M. Sifuentez proudly served for the former U.S. Immigration and Naturalization Service (INS) and U.S. Immigration and Customs Enforcement (ICE) as a federal law enforcement officer. In all, he served as a public servant for over 27 years (14 years in a management or leadership position, including headquarters) before retiring at the end of January of 2020. He obtained his bachelor's degree from the University of Texas at Dallas (UTD) with Cum Laude Honors. A native of Dallas, TX, he now resides in El Paso, TX, with his wife and two younger children.

While serving in a leadership position at the end of his career, apart from enforcing United States immigration law, a large part of his duties called for him to be engaged with the community. This was on full display, when he served as a Deputy Field Office Director, in El Paso, TX, starting in October of 2018. This is when he met with local community representatives and organizations (e.g. El Paso Chief of Police; County Sheriff; City Manager; City Emergency Management Coordinator; numerous U.S. Congressional and Senate Representatives and staff; and local non-governmental organizations, including the two local Catholic Bishops, Baptist and Lutheran ministers, the United Nations High Commission for Refugees (UNHCR), Red Cross and the Child Protection Agency) on a regular basis in town hall style meetings, roundtable discussions and public speaking events to seek their assistance and support during the 2018-2019 southern border humanitarian crisis, which led to the safe release of over 100 thousand migrant family members, including children, to local safe shelters managed by local Non-Governmental Organizations. It also led to him gaining the trust and respect of many of the local community leaders, and helped him develop a healthy relationship and reputation with many of them.

As a proud seventh generation American (second generation on his mother's side) growing up in a modest, low-income, tight-knit community in the southside of Dallas, TX (Oak Cliff), Joe's parents showed him at an early age the importance of taking a lead role in contributing to one's community and performing one's civic duties. For instance, his father served as a deacon minister of the Catholic Church. As such, when Joe was a young boy, besides being named after a Catholic Priest (Father Joe Michael) who was a close friend of his parents, and serving as an altar boy at church , he, along with the rest of his family members, attended many events intended to help those in need in the surrounding Dallas/ Fort Worth area. As an adult, he continues to believe that it is important for him and his family to help others. It is one of the major reasons why he chose to become a public servant, and in line with what he and his spouse, Dora G. Sifuentez (Dorys), are showing their children. His older son is doing his part as a public servant as a legal advisor/attorney for the Capital of The State of Texas, and his younger sons have volunteered to help feed the migrant families at the local shelters and helped at the local Food Bank. His spouse and daughter served as public school teachers.

Joe also believes that it is important to always do the right thing, even when it is not the more popular decision. This was on full display, when he helped the thousands of migrant families in 2018-2019. It was also on full display while he wrote this book, because he knows that some of his former colleagues might not take kindly to some of the changes that he is proposing.

Although his political beliefs coincide more with conservatives, he considers himself to be politically nonbiased, because he bases his vote more on a candidate's political agenda and platform than on the political party. He also considers himself to be one of the federal government's biggest advocate and critic, because after serving for the government for many years, he knows that each Agency has its share of great practices and flaws. ICE is no exception. Moreover, if he ever decides to announce his candidacy to run for a future political position, although he will likely run as a middle of the road Republican, his political agenda will likely be more in line with level-headed, middle of the road/moderate Democrats and Republicans.

Joe considers his biggest thrills in life, besides meeting the love of his life and the birth of his children and grandchildren, were meeting Vice President Pence, Deputy Attorney General Rosenstein, and several members of the U.S. House of Representatives during his federal career; seeing President Bush in person during the 5th Anniversary Celebration of DHS; playing an instrumental role during the humanitarian crisis; being an original member of DHS, when it was created in 2003; working for the federal government for over 27 years; and watching his children blossom into great human beings.

Joe also takes a lot of pride in having several uncles who served during World War II (Pedro Sifuentez – Navy, Julio Alcaraz – Navy,

Joe Flores – Army (Mother's Adopted Brother) and Frank Alcaraz – Army). His Uncle Julio served on the U.S.S. Missouri and was onboard to witness the Japanese surrender to the United States. He also takes a lot of pride in having a family that is truly reflective of the melting pot and exemplifies what the American dream is all about. His wife immigrated to the United States from Mexico, along with her family; his son-in-law is a Jewish descendent; his daughter-in-law is from Germany; and his step-mother is from Venezuela. They are all very productive members of our society. Many of them are now serving in public servant positions or as business owners.

Lastly, those very close to Joe know that he has a successful track record in convincing others of the importance of working hard and smart, always treating others with dignity and respect, and doing your best to keep a positive attitude at all times. It's likely why he has a proven track record in improving employee morale at the field offices that he led.

*This book is dedicated to
my wife, Dorys, my children (Jesse, Vanessa, Dorian and Darien)
and grandchildren (Jessica, Cecilia, Anastasia and Natalie). Thank
you for all the sacrifices you made while I furthered my career as a
public servant. You all bring much joy, love and laughter to my life.
I love you all with all of my heart.*

*It is also dedicated to
the brave and honorable men and women who serve in our law
enforcement and military forces, and their families, for the personal
sacrifices they continuously endure to keep our great country safe.*

INTRODUCTION

Although I agree that the United States Congress is one of the greatest inventions in modern civil society, it has routinely failed to address the decades-long issue regarding the need for immigration reform. As a result, there are now (based on various sources) anywhere from 10.5 to 14.3 million unlawfully present immigrants residing in the United States. Of which, approximately 700,000 are currently in limbo as Deferred Action for Childhood Arrivals (DACA) applicants. To put this in perspective, unlawfully present immigrants make up 3.18 to 4.33 percent of the population in the United States, and DACA recipients less than one percent.

The far-right (overly conservatives) political supporters argue that the United States needs to deport all unlawfully present immigrants, because they are taking American jobs. To the contrary, the far-left (liberals) political supporters argue that the United States needs to open the borders and allow everybody to enter the United States. Anyone with common sense knows that neither of these philosophies or views truly benefits the United States in its traditional and unchanged state, because both of them have several obvious flaws.

The far-right's argument that unlawfully present immigrants are taking American jobs is exaggerated. First, 3.18 to 4.33

is a very small percentage of the overall population, thus they have a minimal impact regarding taking American jobs, and the resulting unemployment rate. Secondly, the vast majority of unlawfully present immigrants seek jobs that are less appealing to most Americans, because they usually seek minimum wage jobs associated to field work or some other type of labor-intensive work.

The far-right also needs to understand that it's an impossible undertaking to remove over 14 million undocumented immigrants from the United States, because ICE only has a finite number of enforcement officers (less than 7,000 deportation officers nationwide). As a result, on average, ICE is only able to carry out 200 to 400 thousand removals each fiscal year. Besides, many mainstream (middle of the road) Americans will argue that this measure is very inhumane, because it will victimize millions of innocent unlawfully present children.

The far-left's argument that the United States needs to open its borders is so far to the left that I find it very difficult to find a way to relate with this way of thinking. In its unchanged state, from a philosophical perspective, just based solely on the sheer number of immigrants that would likely come to the United States, their way of thinking would make this country very vulnerable to terrorist attacks, because it would be impossible for our law enforcement components to keep up with all of the possible threats. As is, it is already near impossible. Then, besides this, once you imagine the mass number of immigrants that will likely come to the United States, you do not need an education lesson from a mathematician or an economist to figure out that this will lead to higher unemployment rates, higher medical premiums, a weaker economy, and less social security benefits to those who are lawfully present.

The far-left supporters also need to remember that the United States is a sovereign country, and like any other sovereign country, has the right to protect its internationally recognized boundaries and the people who legally reside here (U.S. Citizens and Lawful Permanent Residents).

As part of the legislative branch, Congress possesses the legal authority and power to introduce a bill that can end this decades-long immigration debate. Both sides of the House only need to be willing to find a compromise that satisfies both sides.

Unfortunately, our Founders made it easier to block legislation than to enact it. The Government Affairs Institute *at Georgetown University* reported "In a typical two-year Congress, somewhere in the range of 9,000 to 14,000 bills will be introduced, but fewer than 5 percent will become law." As a result, it is difficult for a controversial bill, like immigration reform, to pass the House floor.

In addition, although an idea may come from a variety of sources, only Members of Congress may introduce a piece of legislation. This book is aimed at convincing the Members of Congress to introduce a bi-partisan bill tied to immigration reform that makes sense to both sides of the House, through compromise. Moreover, it's aimed at introducing a bill that assures order and humanity in the immigration process.

CHAPTER 1: EXPAND THE USE OF ATD PROGRAM

In FY 2002, the legacy Immigration and Naturalization Service (INS) created the Alternatives to Detention (ATD) program in pursuant to a Congressional mandate. Specifically, Public Law 107-77, Departments of Commerce, Justice, and State, the Judiciary, and Related Agencies Appropriations Act of 2002, appropriated $3 million for the creation of programs that would help assure that aliens released from detention nevertheless appear for their court hearings. Consequently, since its creation, the program goals for the ATD program have included improving both the compliance with conditions of release for aliens released from ICE custody (including attendance at immigration hearings), and with the execution of final orders of removal. The ATD program uses a variety of tools and/or techniques, including scheduled office visits, unannounced home visits, and electronic monitoring (EM) to accomplish these goals.

Moreover, the ATD program was created, because not every alien taken into ICE custody has to be placed into traditional detention facilities. Low threat and low risk aliens can be placed into a non-traditional setting (e.g. ATD) as they complete their immigration proceedings. In doing so, ICE uses a more cost-effective solution to hardened detention facilities and is able to free up bed space for those aliens who must be detained.

Additionally, the ATD program allows ICE to help CBP release unique populations (e.g. families, non-criminal females, etc.) out of holding cells at the ports and stations, which exponentially frees up their space. For instance, in releasing one family from custody, CBP is able to free up holding cells for 2 and 3 times more individual aliens, because they are able to place more individual adults into a holding cell. Whereas, one family can take up an entire holding cell to themselves.

Currently, ICE considers several factors when determining whether or not to enroll an individual into any ATD program, including but not limited to, basic program eligibility, coverage/service availability of where the person resides, and whether or not there is any space available within the specific program for the person's placement. If no space or service coverage is available in one of these ATD supervision programs, ICE may nevertheless opt to use some form of electronic monitoring. In its conception, the current ATD program, Intensive Supervision Appearance Program (AKA: ISAP), was available in only a few ICE field office locations, however since the commencement of the ISAP II contract in FY 2009, ATD services are now available in all field office locations, and several sub-offices.

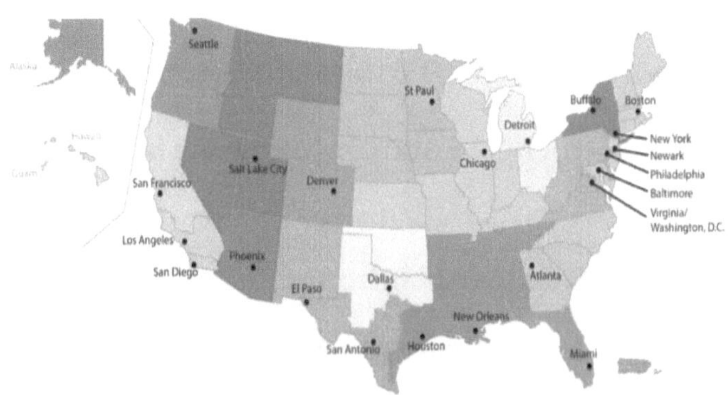

The current ISAP contract also now gives ICE leadership the flexibility to expand the program to other locations without needing to award another contract.

Congress continues to specifically earmark funding for ATD programs as one way of addressing the multitude of issues associated with illegal immigration. Moreover, it has significantly increased the appropriated funds dedicated to ATD. For instance, the ATD program exceeded $180 million in funding, in FY 2019.

However, opportunities exist to better optimize the use of the ATD program on a nationwide basis. Moreover, as more criminal aliens are identified for removal, there arises a greater need to make bed space available for those criminal alien offenders. As such, there arises a greater need to provide an appropriate alternative to detention to unlawfully present non-criminal immigrants.

Using the technology that is currently available, the ATD program has already proven that it can effectively transform historical approaches to ICE's supervision of its non-detained population. As such, it's time to use the ATD program for the vast majority of unlawfully present 'non-criminal' immigrants who are apprehended in the interior of the United States (beyond 100 miles of the Southern border) or released by U.S. Customs and Border Protection (within 100 miles of the Southern Border).

This will greatly benefit ICE and the tax payers of the United States in several ways.

View ICE in a More Positive Light

For decades, the former INS and ICE have been victimized by the left-wing media affiliates, politicians and their advocates' negative rhetoric; because, they believe that detention is obsessive and inhumane for non-criminals. As a result, they view ICE in a negative light. Some of them have gone as far as referring to ICE officers as a bunch of Nazis. Although we know that this is not true, one should not dismiss that they bring up a valid point. Why does ICE continue to lock up non-criminal offenders, when the ATD program has already proven to be an effective alternative? Keep in mind, most politicians do not agree that ICE should discontinue taking all unlawfully present immigrants into custody, because they realize that criminal offenders jeopardize public safety and national security. This is why most of them are in full support of ICE's efforts to continue to target immigrants who have been convicted of a crime, serious enough to reach the level of removal from the United States, or there is probable cause for a reasonable person to believe that a targeted immigrant has committed a crime that meets the threshold of removal from the United States. It's the non-criminals that create all of the commotion, which is also one of the major underlying factors that convinced mayors and governors to institute sanctuary policies that protect unlawfully present immigrants. There stands a good chance that they might be more willing to lift these policies if ICE is willing to only target criminal offenders, and willing to use the ATD program for others. It also might help ICE be viewed in a more positive light.

Cost Savings

The ATD program is a comprehensive array of alternative detention settings and methods that, when employed, will provide a more cost-effective solution to ensuring that low risk individuals in immigration proceedings comply with their immigration obligations.

When times have been tough, ICE has traditionally cut spending in some areas to continue operations within its means. However, in detaining individuals, there is always an inherit risk that unexpected costs will arise due to the associated costs to keep somebody in custody (e.g. medical expenses, associated legal costs, etc.). With ATD, it is less likely that these unexpected costs will arise; because, ATD programs are not a form of custody. As such, ATD participants are required to seek and pay for their own medical care and less likely to file a habeas corpus lawsuit against the government. Thus, with ATD, unexpected costs to the government usually do not arise, therefore there is a far better likelihood to avoid unexpected debt. Besides, the average daily costs for somebody in detention is far over $100. Whereas, the average daily cost for somebody enrolled in ATD is less than $10. Thus, with ATD, the government realizes significant cost savings. Moreover, the savings can be even exponentially more, if the Government opts to place unlawfully present immigrant families into ATD instead of the vastly more expensive family residential centers, which costs over $300 a day for each family member.

Continued High Compliance Rates

Prior to the implementation of ATD, according to a 2003 report by the Office of Inspector General, only 13 percent of ICE's non-detained population complied with their reporting requirements (*See* U.S. Department of Justice, Office of Inspector General, *The Immigration and Naturalization Service's Removal of Aliens Issued Orders, No. 1-2003-004* (Feb. 2003)). With ATD, the overall compliance rate has risen to nearly 80 percent for current ATD, which is a significantly higher than the pre ATD rate of 13 percent. Meaning, the ATD program is effective.

Targeting of Criminal Immigrants

On average, ICE removes between 100 to 200 thousand criminals from the United States each fiscal year. If ICE discontinues targeting non-criminal aliens, starts enrolling the vast majority of the non-criminal encounters into ATD, and discontinues supporting CBP with their custodial responsibilities, ICE should be able to increase its enforcement posture throughout the United States. Moreover, ICE should be able to identify, arrest and remove more criminal removals each fiscal year; which is more in line with the Department's mission in providing public safety and national security. ICE will only need to shift the officers currently assigned to detention responsibilities to its enforcement activities. As force-multipliers, the additional officers should be able to increase the number of criminal arrests.

CHAPTER 2: DEDICATED DOCKET FOR ATD CASES WITH EOIR

Currently, ICE/Enforcement & Removal Operations (ERO) Headquarters' primary ATD program is a community-based supervision and in-person reporting program called ISAP III, which is designed to provide cost-effective alternatives to secure detention for low-risk aliens being released from custody. The program ensures compliance of its participants with the conditions of release, immigration court attendance, voluntary departure, and final orders of removal. It also has an Electronic Monitoring- only (EM-only) component that is available to the participating ICE/ERO offices nationwide.

However, before expanding the use of the ATD program as a cost savings measure, ICE Headquarters somehow needs to reduce that current average length of the individuals enrolled in the various programs in order to make the program cost efficient.

ICE/ERO will be able to significantly reduce the current length of the individuals enrolled in the various ATD programs through a memorandum of understanding with the Department of Justice, Executive Office for Immigration Review (EOIR), that expedites or "fast tracks" ATD participants through the EOIR immigration hearing process. Although ICE and EOIR are meeting regularly to discuss "fast track" approaches for ATD cases, not much headway has occurred due to EOIR's concern that this might affect the prioritization of EOIR's detained case docket. It is believed that a "fast track" for ATD participants will reduce the average length in immigration proceedings, which is currently very lengthy. In addition, it is believed that ICE will be able to double the number of participants that are enrolled into the program each year, if a fast track docket is implemented, which will also likely lead to a significant cost savings to the government due to not needing to place these participants into a costly detention facility. In the event the vast-majority of the non-criminals are enrolled into ATD, it will be critical for ICE/ERO and EOIR to work this out. Congress could play a useful role in resolving the hold up by appropriating EOIR with immigration judges solely for ATD docket purposes.

CHAPTER 3:

IMPLEMENTATION OF KIOSK-TYPE TECHNOLOGY

Although the birth of Kiosk-Type technology (e.g. vending machines) dates as far back as the 1880s, it did not become prevalent worldwide until the 1960s. At which point, the first kiosks that we use today started to emerge. Then, around 1972, the technology exploded in popularity, when the first automated teller machine (ATM) was put into use.

In the 1980s, Kiosk-Type technology continued to evolve, when the Florsheim Shoe Company introduced the first network of interactive kiosks. This advanced, first of its kind, and game changer technology enabled the customers to have their shoes shipped to their homes, after purchasing the shoes using the kiosks.

The interactive kiosk technology started to become prevalent in the government sector in the 2000s. This is when several DHS components started using this technology.

USCIS started using the technology in 2003 to curtail the long lines of people who previously awaited in front of the buildings for hours to schedule an appointment. This is when they introduced InfoPass, which is an online program and website for scheduling appointments through the internet and kiosk-type technology. The technology proved to be successful.

By the end of 2003, USCIS reported nearly 40% of the appointments scheduled were being made through the kiosks. They also reported that during its first six months in operation, the system never crashed. InfoPass revolutionized the way USCIS does business by ending the long appointment lines.

U.S. Customs and Border Protection (CBP) also found that kiosk-type technology adds efficiencies to its operations. For instance, CBP is now testing kiosk-type technology as part of US-VISIT's exit component to verify the departure of visitors that come to the United States. They are also now using self-service automated passport control (APC) kiosks to improve its U.S. preclearance process in other countries. This has allowed passengers to pass through the necessary pre-clearance process in a speedier manner, because the passengers are able to scan their passports for identification, with fingerprint validation and a camera on the kiosk which captures their facial biometrics. This advanced biometric technology has helped CBP to process passengers securely in less than 60 seconds.

Unfortunately, ICE is behind the curve in taking advantage of this advanced technology. Moreover, it's time for ICE to start utilizing kiosk-type technology as part of its operations, because it is long overdue. With continuous budget cuts in the horizon, and the slim chance that ICE will receive additional officer positions in the future, ICE needs to start using this type of technology as an extra security measure and force-multiplier, as soon as possible.

Instead of reinventing the wheel, ICE could emulate some of the other Agencies' kiosk-type technology that is already being utilized within the Department. For instance, ICE could greatly benefit in emulating the APC's advanced biometric technology to quickly cross reference a person's immigration and criminal history, as part of its noncustodial responsibilities, when a person is required to report to an ICE office.

In doing so, the kiosk-type technology will serve as a force-multiplier, because it will augment the officers normally used to support the reporting requirements for those individuals who are released from custody, but still have to periodically report to an office as part of the conditions of release that need to be met. Thus, it will reduce the number of officers now needed to fulfill this responsibility.

Moreover, the kiosk-type technology will be beneficial to all parties, because the participants will be able to fulfill their reporting requirements without always having to go through the stressful and sometimes intimidating experience of having to see an ICE officer. ICE offices will significantly benefit from this technology, because the field offices each have large numbers of aliens who have been ordered removed, but cannot be removed in the foreseeable future (Zadvydas v. Davis, 533 U.S. 678) and are currently reporting in person to deportation officers nationwide. The Kiosk initiative will assist the field offices with the reporting requirements of these types of individuals. In addition, kiosk-type technology could be used for non-criminals who are currently in immigration proceedings. In doing so, the kiosk biometric reporting method will allow the officers to control the supervision of these individuals while reducing the in-person reporting requirements. ICE will then have the latitude and flexibility to assign the officers to other duties, such as: identifying, arresting and removing criminals; issuing General Call-in-Letters (G-56) to check on the status of an individual; and augmenting CBP operations along the Southwest border.

CHAPTER 4: PERMIT CBP TO ACQUIRE ERO IN THE SOUTHWEST BORDER

In response to the September 11, 2001 attacks, President George W. Bush announced the establishment of the Office of Homeland Security (OHS) to coordinate "homeland security" efforts. As per public knowledge, the OHS was intended to develop and coordinate the implementation of a comprehensive national strategy to secure the United States from terrorist threats or attacks, and coordinate the executive branch's efforts to detect, prepare for, prevent, protect against, respond to, and recover from terrorist attacks within the United States.

As part of the passage of the Homeland Security Act by Congress in November 2002, the U.S. Department of Homeland Security (DHS) formally came into being as a stand-alone, Cabinet-level department to further coordinate and unify national homeland security efforts, opening its doors on March 1, 2003.

According to border theorist Peter Andreas, "the creation of DHS constituted the most significant government reorganization since the Cold War, and the most substantial reorganization of federal agencies since the National Security Act of 1947, which placed the different military departments under a secretary of defense and created the National Security Council and Central Intelligence Agency. The creation of DHS also constituted the most diverse merger of federal functions and responsibilities, incorporating 22 government agencies into a single organization."

The following agencies were created within DHS as a result of the merger of the 22 Agencies:

<u>U.S. Citizenship and Immigration Service:</u> Processes and examines citizenship, residency, and asylum requests from aliens.

<u>U.S. Customs and Border Protection:</u> Law enforcement agency that enforces U.S. laws along its international borders (air, land, and sea) including its enforcement of U.S. immigration, customs, and agriculture laws while at and patrolling between all U.S. ports-of-entry.

<u>U.S. Immigration and Customs Enforcement:</u> Law enforcement agency divided into two components:

1.   **Homeland Security Investigations (HSI)** investigates

violations of more than 400 U.S. laws and gathers intelligence on national and international criminal activities that threaten the security of the homeland; and

2.   **Enforcement and Removal Operations (ERO)** enforces administrative violations of the Immigration and Nationality Act by detaining, deporting, and removing violators of United States immigration law.

Transportation Security Administration: Responsible for aviation security (domestic and international, most notably conducting passenger screenings at airports), as well as land and water transportation security.

U.S. Coast Guard: Military service responsible for law enforcement, maritime security, national defense, maritime mobility, and protection of natural resources.

U.S. Secret Service: Law enforcement agency tasked with two distinct and critical national security missions:

1. Investigative Mission - The investigative mission of the USSS is to safeguard the payment and financial systems of the United States from a wide range of financial and electronic-based crimes.

2.   Protective Mission - The protective mission of the USSS is to ensure the safety of the President of the United States, the Vice President of the United States, and their immediate families, and foreign heads of state.

Federal Emergency Management Agency: Agency that oversees the federal government's response to natural disasters like earthquakes, hurricanes, tornadoes, floods, forest fires.

Although the creation of DHS took several critical steps in the right direction regarding adding more structure and coordination amongst the components and in reducing communication gaps with respect to intelligence, in hindsight, the dismantling and reorganization of the former INS components should have been distributed slight differently. Moreover, ERO and HSI should not have been merged within the same Agency. Instead, the investigative duties of the former INS and U.S. Customs Service should have fallen within its own Agency, when HSI was created. The detention and removal responsibilities within the former INS should have been split within two separate DHS Agencies; within 100 miles of the Southern border, the former assets, including the personnel, should have been placed within CBP, and outside of 100 miles of the Southern border, should have been placed within its own respective Agency.

For instance, ICE/ ERO's San Antonio Field Office (SNA), although located in San Antonio, TX, provides support to 19 CBP Ports of Entry by land, sea and air and 3 Border Patrol Sectors; and 430 miles of border from the western most jurisdictions in Del Rio to the southernmost tip of the United States in Brownsville (The following map displays ERO San Antonio Field Office's AOR).

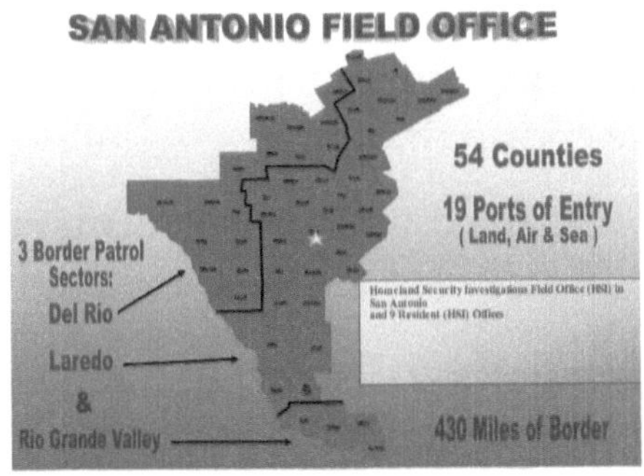

As a result, SNA's Field Office Director's permanent duty location is very distant from a large part of the officers and support staff and most of the mission critical activities that are occurring on a daily basis along the Southwest border. For example, the Rio Grande Valley (RGV) is approximately four (4) hours away from the SNA Field Office (via automobile). This is concerning, because SNA's Harlingen Resident Office (HRO) and Port Isabel Detention Center (PIDC) are also located in the RGV. This equates to over 300 employees, which is more employees than some of the small ICE/ERO field offices have on board. This is also concerning, because:

1. CBP's leadership's duty station is located in the RGV.

2. The RGV is routinely the targeted area of the influx of intended immigrants that are attempting to enter the United States illegally.

3. A large part of the Cartel activity is occurring along the RGV Southwest border.

4. One of ICE/ERO's Service Processing Centers (SPC), PIDC, is located in the RGV, which serves as the primary conduit for the intake of all CBP's apprehensions in the RGV.

5. HRO oversees a juvenile unit, family unit, non-detained (Bonds and ATD), at-large fugitive operations, and the intake of criminal immigrants from local, state and federal facilities within an area covering 251 miles of international border with Mexico, and Cameron, Willacy, Hidalgo, and Starr, TX counties. These four counties encompass approximately 4,300 square miles.

6. HRO also supports 11 CBP ports of entry, eight (8) Border Patrol stations, two (2) Border Patrol check points and one (1) Border Patrol Sector office in coordinating the transportation and placement of juveniles, family units and adult females.

7. Routinely, most of the unaccompanied children (UAC) and family members apprehended by CBP occurs in the RGV.

This is an awful lot of responsibility for offices distant from a field office. To simplify operations, and make the infrastructure more structurally and logistically feasible, this part of SNA's current area of responsibility could be acquired by CBP since it is within 100 miles of the Southwest border. The same concept could be applied to the ERO El Paso, Phoenix and San Diego Field Office.

Obviously, it will now take an Act of Congress to do this. It will also require that CBP be given the legal authority to exercise custodial determinations (Covered in Chapter 7/Grant Custody Authority to CBP), and a lot of coordination between CBP and ICE; because, CBP will need to learn the ins and outs of detention management (e.g. detention standards, dealing with inspections and oversight, etc.), before assuming this responsibility.

However, despite these challenges, there are several reasons why the changes are well-worth the time and energy to put them into place.

Eliminate the constant complaining and strong-arm tactics between the two agencies

As a former member of the ICE/ERO's leadership team, on numerous occasions, I witnessed CBP and ICE using strong-arm tactics to persuade the other agency to give into some kind of operational change. These confrontations often led to a lot of confusion, frustration, and although the two agencies will never admit it to each other, led to lasting ill-feelings between the two agencies. In addition, these incidents led to ill-advised and unnecessary delays to important projects and operational objectives, because the two agencies often had to wait for their respective headquarters component to get back to them with a decision before moving forward with an unresolved matter. This often led to even more confusion and delays, because the two agencies would then receive conflicting decisions from their respective headquarters. Afterwards, the matter would be elevated to the Secretary of DHS. Meaning, the agencies could not move forward with the unresolved matter until the Secretary made a decision, which sometimes took weeks and months. In the end, the agency with more political will and contacts often would get its way. The other agency would then be basically bullied into accepting the decision. This happened on more than one occasion, when the former Commissioner of CBP became the Acting Secretary of DHS.

Stop casting blame on the other agency

CBP and ICE also often cast blame on each other, when things do not go according to plan. This was on full display during the 2018 southern border surge, when countless number of family members arrived to the Southwest border. As CBP's number of apprehensions increased so did the time in custody of the families and unaccompanied children in CBP's custody. This became legally problematic for CBP once a family or an unaccompanied child reached over 72 hours in their custody due to a court ruling, as a result of the Flores Settlement Court Ruling[1], and CBP not having custodial authority.

As this occurred, CBP often casted blame on ICE for not accepting (transfer of custody) the families in a timely manner (within 24 hours of CBP completing the necessary paperwork). Conversely, ICE would cast blame on CBP, because CBP often failed to process the necessary documents to transfer the families to ICE before the

72-hour threshold. This happened often during the high point of the surge, because it was difficult for the two agencies to keep up with the massive surge. Things would have gone much smoother, and likely speedier, if all of the operational responsibilities (e.g. processing, transfer and custody responsibilities) only fell under one agency.

Negative media attention also added to the casting of blame. For instance, when CBP started separating families in order to prosecute the head of household of the families, the media, and many politicians, spun it as if ICE was separating the families. Although ICE did not play a significant role in separating the families, and actually played a humanitarian role by reuniting the families, it led to a big nationwide push to dismantle the agency. ICE was left to fend for itself, because CBP only made a trivial attempt to accept blame for their politically volatile and unwise decision. The Department also could and should have done a much better job of defending ICE during this crisis. Moreover, as a result of not doing enough, ICE's image will probably never fully recover from this crisis.

Reduce the constant turnover at CBP

It's common knowledge to those who work within the Department that U.S. Border Patrol (USBP) struggles to successfully recruit and keep their agents onboard. This problem has gone on for several years, and predates President Trump's administration.

Although USBP has made improvements in its recruitment and hiring process, each year, they continue to remain under their funded staffing level. Meaning, their number of agent positions onboard has mostly trended downward from one year to another.

One could pinpoint USBP's ongoing recruiting and retention problem on a number of different factors. For instance, it is difficult to recruit qualified applicants from major cities, because remote towns near the Southwest border is not an appealing location for most potential candidates. A lot of the major cities also offer better pay and benefits, and without required shift work.

As for the retention problem, it is widely known that the vast majority of the agents leave USBP to go to ICE. The problem appears to have worsen, when the agents lost administratively uncontrollable overtime (AUO) in 2016, which allowed them to receive overtime pay for work at the end of a shift up to additional 25 percent of their regular salary (See Appendix B/ICE Premium Pay Guide: AUO). They now only receive a set amount of 20 percent of overtime pay, which does not increase for extra hours worked.

ICE ERO Deportation Officers, on the other hand, continue to receive AUO, and additional pay covered under the Fair Labor Standards Act (See Appendix C/ICE Premium Pay Guide: FLSA) and receive time and a half for their overtime hours that are scheduled before the current work week. In addition, Deportation Officers mostly work a standard Monday through Friday day shift and in a controlled indoor environment located in a major metropolitan area, including along the Southwest border. Whereas, USBP agents are required to work in rural locations; night shifts; extremely cold, hot and rainy weather; and on weekends and holidays.

As an overtime compromise, in the event the merger is approved,

Congress might also want to consider changing the overtime pay to Law Enforcement Availability Pay (LEAP), which would limit the overtime cap to 25 percent of the officer's regular salary (See Appendix D/ICE Premium Pay Guide: LEAP). It would basically serve as a happy medium regarding overtime pay, because it would increase the Border Patrol Agents' overtime pay by five percent (currently 20 percent cap) and continue to give the current ERO Deportation Officers the 25 percent overtime pay cap that they are receiving, but with no FLSA pay. The Department has been pushing for this overtime change since President Obama's administration was in charge. This is when Congress and the Department made a push to discontinue AUO and FLSA as a method to compensate the Border Patrol Agents and the Deportation Officers for their extra hours worked.

Force-multiplier for CBP

Besides reducing the constant turnover of USBP Agents leaving CBP, the merger will also serve as a force-multiplier for the agency, because USBP will acquire hundreds of officers and thousands of contractor staff as part of the merger. For instance, in the El Paso, TX proper alone, USBP will acquire over 200 officers and 1,000 contractor staff. The officers can be used to serve in a variety of duties while the contractor staff can continue to be used to oversee the facilities.

Easy transition because a large percentage of ERO officers along the Southwest border are former USBP agents

According to CBP statistics, Border Patrol agents consistently leave their agency for other law enforcement agencies, such as Immigration and Customs Enforcement (ICE). As a result, for fiscal years 2013 through 2017, actual retirements accounted for less than a quarter of annual Border Patrol agent losses, indicating that the majority of these agents are not retiring but are generally leaving to pursue other employment. Further, according to CBP data, the number of Border Patrol agents departing for employment at other federal agencies increased steadily, from 75 agents in fiscal year 2013 to 348 agents in fiscal year 2017 —or nearly 40 percent of all Border Patrol agent losses in that fiscal year. Many of them went to the ICE/ERO Field Offices along the Southwest border, which is a trend that the Department recognizes has continued through the years. With this in mind, it should not be a difficult transition to merge the two agencies, because many of the officers (former USBP agents) should already be familiar with USBP operations. Thus, the training requirements to complete the transition should be minimal.

CHAPTER 5:
BREAKUP OF ICE

For several years, advocacy groups and members of Congress have been very vocal about dismantling ICE. The big push came, when ICE was falsely accused of separating families along the Southwest border. Although CBP created and executed the operational decision to separate families in order to prosecute a parent(s) for attempting to unlawfully enter the United States, it was ICE who received the brunt of the negative media attention, when CBP executed the plan. This resulted in a big push to do away with the agency. The lingering effect from this push continues today.

Although ICE's public affairs office and leadership have made an honest attempt to try to overcome the negative attention that the agency has drawn over the years, it's now obvious that the Agency will never be able to free itself from this insurmountable negativity. As a result, the Agency will continue to be viewed in a negative light and its image will likely be tarnished indefinitely. Moreover, the Agency will never receive the gratitude and respect that it deserves for doing its part to protect our communities and great nation.

Now knowing that ICE's image is likely beyond repair, it's time that the Agency accept this and move forward in making some significant changes. Moreover, it's time for Congress and the Department to work collectively to make significant structural changes to the Agency.

Allow HSI to Become its own Agency

In 2018, collectively, the majority of HSI Special Agents in Charge submitted a memorandum to DHS Secretary Kirstjen Nielsen proposing the separation of HSI and ERO. They wrote "ERO has become very effective and efficient at detaining and removing illegal aliens. HSI, now the second largest federal investigative agency, has become the U.S. Government's 'Transnational Investigative' agency, plugging the gap between more domestically-focused federal law enforcement and the international sources and methods of crime that significantly impact the U.S. The two ICE sub-agencies have become so specialized and independent that ICE's mission can no longer be described as a singular synergistic mission; it can only be described as a combination of the two distinct missions (i.e. 'Enforcement/Removal and Transnational Investigations').

Considering E.O. 13773[2] and the fact that we believe that ICE has reached a point of final maturation in its continued evolution, we propose to restructure ICE into the two separate, independent entities of HSI and ERO."

Besides the points noted in the previous paragraph, it would benefit HSI to have its own distinct mission separate from ERO, because they can then receive their own appropriations each fiscal year and make it easier for them to articulate their specific mission to their stakeholders. In addition, the separation should help them curtail the negative press and lack of cooperation that they are receiving from some of their stakeholders, as a result of the state and local partners, as well as Congressional staff, confusing them for ERO; because, their mission is currently intertwined with ERO's, which are both under the ICE umbrella.

Rebrand ERO

Since the inception of ICE, members of Congress, ICE's stakeholders, its employees and the general public have not fully embraced or supported the name. Moreover, many continue to make jokes about the name of the agency. I still recall, when I was deployed to Gulfport, MS to assist with the Hurricane Katrina relief effort, the ridicule we repeatedly underwent, because many of the members of the community and the some of the law enforcement officers from the other agencies made jokes about the name. One of the most popular joke involved a question they asked us; "Why do you need a gun to protect ICE?" Yes, it was humiliating.

Sadly, even though the officers in the field continue to be ridiculed for the name, ICE leadership has not been willing to change the name. Moreover, it's obvious that not much research or thought was done before the name of the Agency was rolled out. Otherwise, I'm convinced that the push to name the Agency ICE would have experienced a major meltdown. Sorry, I had to say it; it was too tempting. However, with all jokes set aside, it's no wonder that ICE's survey scores for employee morale is always near the very bottom amongst all of the other federal government agencies.[3]

In addition, let's not forget the insurmountable negative attention that the Agency is currently drawing. This is why ICE must rebrand its name. To simplify the process, I suggest to change the name to Enforcement and Removal Operations (ERO) for continuity. However, although it will take more effort and monies, I believe that the most logical course of action will be for the Agency to sever itself from the ICE name and origin all together. It needs to hit the refresh button. With this being said, I highly recommend that ICE change its name to the 'Interior Enforcement Agency.'[4] After the rebranding, the new Agency can then be assigned the interior immigration enforcement activities beyond one hundred miles of the Southwest border. Simultaneously, CBP can acquire the immigration enforcement activities currently assigned to ICE/ERO that fall within one hundred miles of the Southwest border.

Split OPLA

Once ICE is broken up, ICE's Office of Principal Legal Advisor (OPLA) will need to follow suit. If Congress agrees to place ERO under CBP along the Southwest border, I believe that it would behoove the Department to place each of the current ICE Chief

Counsel and Deputy Chief Counsel along the Southwest border under HSI. Then, place half of the Southwest border ICE legal advisors under CBP and the other half under HSI.

As for the interior part of the United States, once again, it would behoove the Department to split the legal advisors amongst the two agencies. As for the current ICE Chief Counsel and Deputy Chief Counsel supporting the current ERO Field Offices and HSI SAC Offices, I believe the wise decision to make is to split up the Chiefs and Deputy Chiefs evenly amongst the two agencies, and then create new Chief and Deputy Chief positions for the remaining locations that are required to forfeit the positions as a result of the split.

Split IHSC

Like OPLA, there will be a need to split up the ICE Health Service Corps (IHSC), because there will continue to be a need to provide the necessary medical care to the detainees at the facilities. This split should be much easier to execute than OPLA's, if my recommended model regarding merging ERO with CBP along the Southwest border is followed. It will simplify the split, because the hundred-mile threshold can then be used to determine which staff remains with ERO and which goes to CBP. Within the hundred-mile threshold, the IHSC staff will go to CBP. All others will remain with ERO, except in ICE Headquarters. The Department will need to be tasked to determine some kind of even split of IHSC staff at the Headquarters level.

Rollout an effective campaign to introduce the new Agency

An effective campaign plan has an engaging, shareable,

campaign concept that utilizes both online and offline marketing communications tools and digital media channels. When ICE was created, it's obvious that ICE Headquarters' Office of Public Affairs (OPA) failed to roll out an effective campaign to introduce ICE to its stakeholders and the general public. As a result, the vast majority of the general public have never truly understood ICE's mission. Moreover, many of them do not even know that ERO stands for Enforcement and Removal Operations. Thus, they are clueless as to ERO's mission. Then, to add insult to injury, Congressional Representatives and organizations at odds with the Agency have used this to their advantage, because they go to the media regularly to spread false information and rhetoric about the Agency, which benefits their campaigns and political platforms. Many members of the general public will then take their word as gospel, because ICE has failed to educate them.

To prevent the aforementioned false propaganda about the Agency from happening again, Congress and the Department need to work collectively in rolling out an effective campaign to introduce the new Agency. Moreover, before and during the introduction of the new Agency, the new Agency's OPA needs to roll out a proactive media campaign using numerous social media platforms. And, for it to be truly effective, it needs to include media affiliates at the national and all of the local locations nationwide. It also needs to do a far better job than ICE of educating the general public as to the name and mission of the new Agency so the general public will have a better understanding of what the Agency does and hopefully a better appreciation.

CHAPTER 6: DEVELOP THE INFRASTRUCTURE IN THE SOUTHWEST BORDER

Although it is estimated that the federal lands along the Southwest border are owned by five different federal agencies[5], USBP has access to hundreds of miles of federal lands, as a result of a memorandum of understanding (MOU) signed by DHS, the Department of Agriculture, and the Department of Interior on border security. In addition, through Congress, the DHS Secretary has broadened authority to take action on federal lands to secure the border. The DHS Secretary can choose to use this authority to develop the needed infrastructure along the Southwest border, which is long overdue.

Place all of the transportation requirements under one contractor

Upon the merger of CBP and ERO, CBP needs to place all of its transportation requirements along the Southwest border under one contractor. Currently, USBP is only receiving limited contractor support to help them with their transportation needs (e.g. transport their apprehensions to the stations), because the vast majority of the transports are being conducted by their agents.

As for ERO, they currently utilize a multitude of contractors to assist them with this need. In El Paso alone, four contractors are used to fulfill this requirement, with each of them having varying costs and their own jurisdiction, which often leads to a lot of confusion as to which contractor is required to fulfill the need.

With the use of only one contractor, CBP should be able to control its transportation costs more efficiently (save monies) and provide the needed support to the officers and agents in a structured manner. At a minimum, it could improve the communication between the contractor and the agency, because CBP will only need to turn to one contractor for support.

Place the detention facilities along the Southwest border

At times, especially during Southern border surges, ICE has used more than 200 nationwide facilities to detain unlawfully present immigrants who are in proceedings or awaiting to be removed from the United States. Moreover, according to federal government data from April 2019, "Texas (14,481), Louisiana (4,415), Arizona (4,405), California (4,353), and Georgia (3,719), are the top five states with the largest number of people in U.S. immigration detention per day."

The federal government data also reflects that "over 70 percent of people are held in privately-run immigrant prison", with GEO Group receiving more taxpayer dollars for immigration detention than any other ICE contractor. For instance, in FY 2017, GEO Group received $184 million. It was followed by Corrections Corporation of America/CoreCivic that received $135 million. The following chart (Compiled by the Freedom For Immigrants Non-governmental Organization) will give you a more in-depth breakdown of the monies received by the top immigration related contractors.

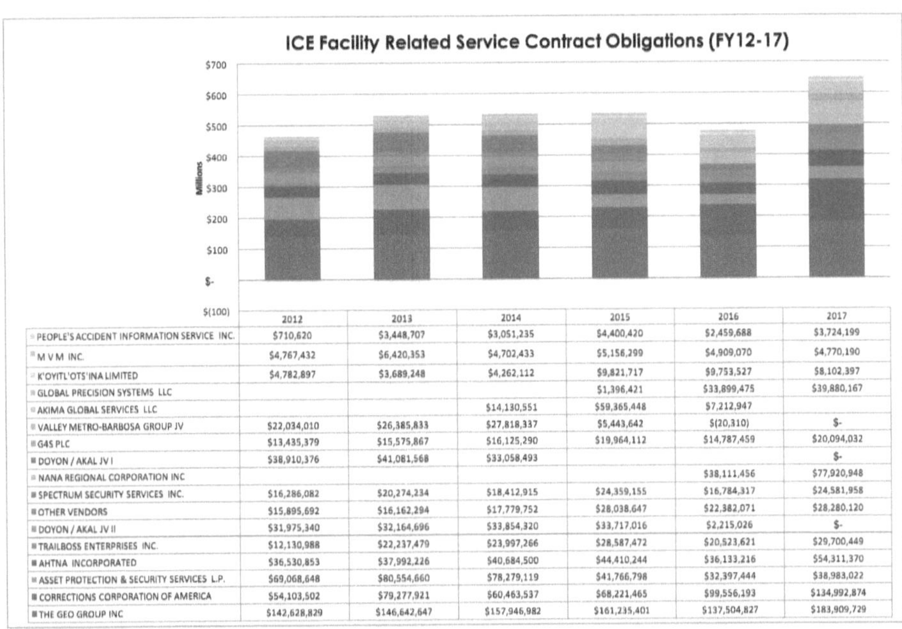

ICE Facility Related Service Contract Obligations (FY12-17)

	2012	2013	2014	2015	2016	2017
PEOPLE'S ACCIDENT INFORMATION SERVICE INC.	$710,620	$3,448,707	$3,051,235	$4,400,420	$2,459,688	$3,724,199
M V M INC.	$4,767,432	$6,420,353	$4,702,433	$5,156,299	$4,909,070	$4,770,190
K'OYITL'OTS'INA LIMITED	$4,782,897	$3,689,248	$4,262,112	$9,821,717	$9,753,527	$8,102,397
GLOBAL PRECISION SYSTEMS LLC				$1,396,421	$33,899,475	$39,880,167
AKIMA GLOBAL SERVICES LLC			$14,130,551	$59,365,448	$7,212,947	
VALLEY METRO-BARBOSA GROUP JV	$22,034,010	$26,385,833	$27,818,337	$5,443,642	$(20,310)	$-
G4S PLC	$13,435,379	$15,575,867	$16,125,290	$19,964,112	$14,787,459	$20,094,032
DOYON / AKAL JV I	$38,910,376	$41,081,568	$33,058,493			$-
NANA REGIONAL CORPORATION INC					$38,111,456	$77,920,948
SPECTRUM SECURITY SERVICES INC.	$16,286,082	$20,274,234	$18,412,915	$24,359,155	$16,784,317	$24,581,958
OTHER VENDORS	$15,895,692	$16,162,294	$17,779,752	$28,038,647	$22,382,071	$28,280,120
DOYON / AKAL JV II	$31,975,340	$32,164,696	$33,854,320	$33,717,016	$2,215,026	$-
TRAILBOSS ENTERPRISES INC.	$12,130,988	$22,237,479	$23,997,266	$28,587,472	$20,523,621	$29,700,449
AHTNA INCORPORATED	$36,530,853	$37,992,226	$40,684,500	$44,410,244	$36,133,216	$54,311,370
ASSET PROTECTION & SECURITY SERVICES L.P.	$69,068,648	$80,554,660	$78,279,119	$41,766,798	$32,397,444	$38,983,022
CORRECTIONS CORPORATION OF AMERICA	$54,103,502	$79,277,921	$60,463,537	$68,221,465	$99,556,193	$134,992,874
THE GEO GROUP INC	$142,628,829	$146,642,647	$157,946,982	$161,235,401	$137,504,827	$183,909,729

To utilize privately-run facilities, ICE must negotiate costs with the local authorities (e.g. local Sheriffs) and government contractors. This results in varying costs amongst the facilities, with some being much more expensive than others.

In addition, since labor costs make up approximately 70 percent of all facility costs[6], it plays an instrumental role in the costs varying amongst the detention facilities, especially since the Service Contract Act (SCA) of 1965 limits ICE's ability to negotiate labor rates in its detention and ground transportation contracts. Besides the SCA, the facility's design and physical layout affect the number of staff needed to monitor the facility, therefore affects the facility's labor cost. For instance, the older facilities usually require more staff, because the outdated layout usually has more blind spots.

Other contributing factors that affect the cost are the distance between the facility and other associated locations (e.g. immigration courts, other nearby competing detention facilities, etc.) and the geographic location of the facility. The facilities located in the northern part of the United States are typically more expensive than the southern facilities.

To further complicate the cost matter, during crisis situations (e.g. Southern border surge), the local authorities often raise the normal bed space rate, because they know that once the surge is over ICE will discontinue using their facility. This sometimes requires ICE to pay ridiculously high bed rates during a surge.

The use of nationwide facilities to support the Southwest border also leads to complicated and confusing transportation issues and very expensive transportation costs, because as noted previously, ICE currently utilizes numerous transportation contractors with varying costs and are required to bus and/or fly detainees all over the country once bed space is available in a particular location. The was an ongoing occurrence at the ERO Atlanta Field Office during the 2018 surge. Although ERO Atlanta's facilities are thousands of miles from San Diego, CA, ERO Atlanta often accepted many of San Diego's detainees as bed space became available. Besides having to burden the very expensive cost of flying the detainees from one side of the country to the other, which ICE reports each daily scheduled charter flight averages $8,577 per flight hour, ICE grew accustom to dealing with frustrating delays associated with air travel (i.e. flight cancelled or postponed due to mechanical issues), as a result of having to use the aircrafts to transport the detainees.

With this being said, to make detention operations more efficient and less costly, the Department, through Congress, needs to use the land available through the MOU with the other agencies to build its own facilities to support 'all' of CBP's detention requirements along the Southwest border.

In conjunction with using only one transportation contractor, the Department should only use one contractor to manage all of the detention facilities along the Southwest border, or at a minimum, one contractor for each Sector.

I also highly suggest that CBP place one 10,000 bed detention facility at each USBP Sector, and each with a guarantee minimum (GM) rate at 30 percent capacity. This will give the contractor the financial stability that it is seeking to do business with the federal government and incentivize the need for them to scale back on their costs when there is a low in activity along the border.

Following the proposed structure will negate the need to transfer detainees to the interior part of the United States and pay varying bed space costs due to using the interior facilities and numerous contractors. Moreover, it will result in a significant savings to the tax payers, because the Department will be able to cut back on the use of aircraft transportation and be able to negotiate one standard bed space and transportation cost rate with a contractor. It will also help the Department manage its bed space more efficiently, because it will only need to coordinate detention and transportation requirements with only one contractor. This will also significantly reduce the delays to transport detainees due to practically eliminating the need to transfer the detainees by aircraft, which currently delays the process up to a week.

Place Family Residential Centers and Office of Refugee Resettlement Shelters in each USBP Sector along the Southwest border

In the same spirit of placing a detention facility at each USBP Sector, DHS/CBP and the U.S. Department of Health and Human Services (HHS)/Office of Refugee Resettlement (ORR)[7] should work with Congress to build Family Residential Centers (FRCs) and ORR shelters at each USBP Sector to accommodate the placement of the vast majority of immigrant families and unaccompanied alien children (UAC) entering the Southwest border.

In addition, as a measure to reduce the possibility of separating families, which caused a political uproar during the last border surge, I highly suggest that DHS/CBP and HHS/ORR agree to build shelters that will merge the current FRC and ORR requirements into one shelter location at each sector. Moreover, in order to circumvent the current legal challenges tied to keeping families in custody, I think that it will be best to dismantle the very flawed traditional FRC structure, and instead, build each ORR shelter adjacent to facilities dedicated solely for the parents and adult siblings of the families. In doing so, the families may be kept together in a controlled yet humane environment.

I also suggest that contractors and ORR staff members be used to provide the necessary oversight at the ORR shelter and adjacent facilities, and like the detention facilities, have one contractor oversee all of the shelters and adjacent facilities at each USBP Sector along the Southwest border. This arrangement is in line with the March 1, 2003, Section 462, Homeland Security Act of 2002, which transferred functions under U.S. immigration laws regarding the care and placement of unaccompanied alien children (UAC) from the Commissioner of the Immigration and Naturalization Service to the Director of the Office of Refugee Resettlement (ORR). Congress will only need to tweak this section of law to allow ORR to also care for and place accompanied alien children (AAC) who are a member of an apprehended family.

The corresponding contract can mirror the capacity requirements of the detention facilities along the Southwest border, which is noted above, except there will be separate custody requirements for the ORR shelter and the adjacent facilities.

Moreover, I highly suggest that CBP and ORR agree to place one 10,000 bed ORR Shelter for UAC and AAC (10 years of age and above); one 5,000 bed facility for adults (2,500 for females and

2,5000 for males) and AAC (under the age of 10); and one 5,000 bed facility for adults (2,500 for females and 2,500 for males) who only have AAC (10 years of age and above) that will be placed in the ORR Shelter. A common area also needs to be incorporated into the plan so to allow all of the family members to be together during the daytime hours.

In addition, like the recommended detention facilities setup mentioned previously, the ORR Shelter and the adjacent adult and AAC facilities need to have a GM rate at 20 percent capacity so to give the contractor the financial stability that it is seeking to do business with the federal government and incentivize the need for them to scale back on their costs when there is a low in activity along the border.

This proposed setup should serve to indirectly disrupt smuggling activities and significantly reduce transportation costs, because under the current setup, UACs are flown to different parts of the country (e.g. Chicago, Los Angeles, Miami, etc.) to place them in a shelter, and then released to a sponsor, who, at times, is a smuggler posing as a sponsor. Thus, at a minimum, besides saving tax payer monies, this new arrangement should help the Department disrupt smuggling activities on the back end by no longer needing to facilitate the transfer of UAC from one location to another, which currently works to the benefit of illegal smuggling organizations.

Place Aircraft Hubs in each USBP Sector

Currently, the twenty-four ERO field offices coordinate with ICE Air Operations, based in Mesa, Arizona, to schedule removal travel and/or domestic transfer via commercial airlines or charter aircraft. ICE uses five ICE Air Operations locations throughout the United States: San Antonio and Brownsville, Texas; Alexandria, Louisiana; Miami, Florida; and Mesa, Arizona.

ICE Air Operations locations also have the ability to conduct removal missions to Central American countries such as Guatemala, El Salvador and Honduras, the Caribbean and South America, and conduct special high-risk charter missions to Europe, Asia, and Africa or to anywhere in the world.

In the event that Congress agrees to give CBP their own custodial authority, as part of this authority, CBP should start conducting their own transfer and removal flights. Moreover, each USBP Sector, through their CBP Headquarters and the formal acquisition process, should be given their own dedicated aircrafts and Hub, and authority to manage their own removal flights to Central America, because the Sectors make up the vast majority of the Central America nationals that are currently being removed. They can also use the aircrafts to conduct special high-risk charter missions, like ICE is currently doing.

In addition, to help the Sectors manage their bed space usage efficiently, the Department and CBP Headquarters should give the Sectors the latitude to coordinate necessary domestic detainee transfers with each other, when transfers are needed amongst Sectors. This should help them streamline the transfers in a timelier manner, which is critical during a border surge.

This change will require a lot of coordination between CBP and ICE before CBP can assume this responsibility, because it will be a very heavy lift for CBP to adopt. Besides the challenge of needing to acquire the needed resources to support the Air Operations (e.g. aircrafts, creation of Hubs, staff, etc.), CBP will need to go through a massive learning curve before ICE can transfer this responsibility to them due to the numerous domestic and international agreements, guidelines, procedures, regulations, and laws that will need to be satisfied (e.g. Airport approval, contractual requirements, FAA regulations, international agreements, venue issues, etc.).

Place Central Processing Centers in each USBP Sector

During the FY 2018 Southern border surge, CBP experienced extremely high capacity and time in custody issues at the Ports and Stations due to the massive number of incoming cases. This led to overcrowded holding cells at the Ports and Stations, because the USBP Agents and CBP Officers couldn't process the cases quickly enough to keep up with the flow. In addition, the Ports and Stations were not constructed to take in such an overwhelming number of cases.

To further complicate the matter, in FY 2018, a high percentage of CBP's apprehensions involved immigrant families and unaccompanied children. This unique challenge proved to be insurmountable, because CBP had very little holding cell space to place the families and the children. This resulted in families and children being placed in overcrowded situations, which triggered a huge uproar from many activists, our politicians, and the local and national media affiliates. I still recall the photographs that depicted the overcrowding situation. I also remember the articles depicting USBP as being inhumane, because they were holding children in overcrowded cells. It also placed CBP in a legal bind, because they violated the Flores Settlement[8] on numerous occasions due to the overwhelming flow, which required them to transfer custody of immigrant families and unaccompanied children to ICE or ORR within 72 hours.

Another hold up during the border surge was that CBP had to wait on a bed space to become available at the detention facilities, the family residential center, or a local shelter before they could make arrangements to transfer a person or family out of the Port or Station, which also led to very frustrating delays.

To prevent these overcrowding situations from occurring again in the future, Congress and the Department need to agree to build central processing centers (CPCs) at each of the USBP Sectors with the capacity to temporarily hold up to 5,000 detainees. This will allow CBP to move persons and families from their Ports and Stations in a timely manner, because they will no longer need to medically screen and process at the Ports and Stations. Instead, this will take place at the CPC. They will also no longer need to wait for a bed space to become available before moving a person or family out of the Ports and Stations, thus significantly reducing the current impact at these locations.

Besides benefiting CBP from an operational standpoint, the development of the infrastructure will help the Department in overcoming some of its current legal challenges and costs, and benefit the local communities along the Southwest border.

Reduce Venue Issues

For various reasons, DHS sometimes relocates detainees after charging documents have been filed. The Immigration Court does not automatically change venue, however, when DHS moves a detainee to a location outside the administrative control of the court where the case is pending. Further, the DHS filing a Form I-830[9], by itself, does not constitute a motion for change of venue (COV). If DHS fails to produce a detainee because that detainee has been moved to another location, the Immigration Court retains venue and administrative control over the case. If DHS produces the detainee at a court in another location, absent a valid order changing venue or a new charging document, venue and administrative control does not reside at that location, except for bond redetermination requests, if any. However, this does not preclude the detainee or the detainee's legal representative from filing a motion to change venue once the detainee is moved to a detention location outside the administrative control of the court where the case is otherwise pending.

In 2018, the Executive Office for Immigration Review (EOIR) and several immigration attorneys expressed their concerns, disagreements and frustrations with ICE as a result of the vast amount of COV cases that occurred that year due to the Southwest border surge. Because of the significant amount of incoming cases that year, bed space quickly became very scarce along the Southwest border. As a result, daily transfers to other locations (i.e. El Paso, TX to Atlanta, GA) practically became a daily occurrence. It then required ICE ERO and OPLA to scramble to give the detainees' legal representatives and EOIR a last-minute notification of the transfer. Obviously, these numerous transfers caused a lot of confusion and chaos for all of the respective parties.

The development of the infrastructure along the Southwest border should work to curtail the need to transfer detainees to other locations, and reduce the number of COV cases, because there will be an adequate number of beds at the local facility to fulfill the need.

Significantly Reduce Costs Tied to Domestic Transfers

In a study conducted by the Henry M Jackson School of International Studies, they calculated that ICE Air Operations flew approximately 1.73 million detainees on nearly 15,000 flight missions in an eight-year span (October 1, 2010 to December 5, 2018). In addition, they found that 28.78% of the flights involved internal/domestic transfers, whereby approximately 500,000 detainees were being moved from one location to another within the United States on a little over 4,300 flights (4,317). The following "ICE Air: annual passengers, removals plus transfer" chart provides an overall breakdown of the missions.

Meaning, if you multiply the daily scheduled charter flight average cost per flight hour of $8,577 times the number of domestic flights in the eight year span of 4,317, and then multiply that sum of $37,026,909 times an average flight hour of 5, which is a conservative number, you will find that the Department could have saved almost 200 million dollars ($185,134,545) of tax payer monies in the eight year span by doing away with the domestic transfers, which is a significant savings.

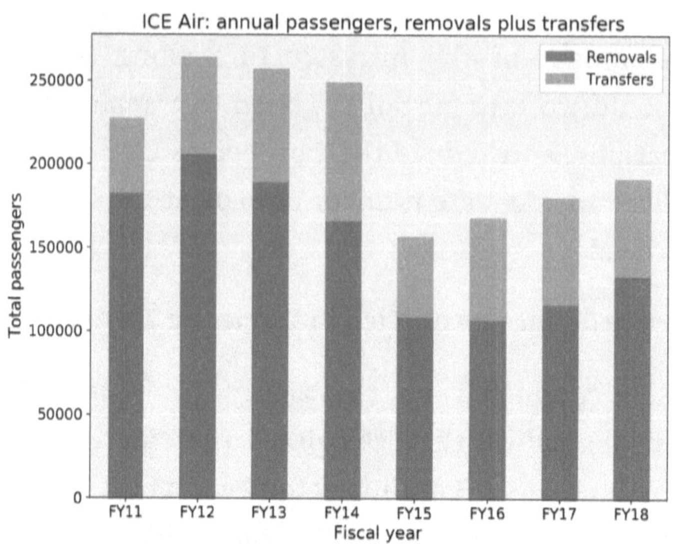

Create new jobs

The detainee-to-staff ratio for ICE detention facilities currently has a national average of 3.1 to 1. Thus, in the event Congress and the Department agree to the proposed plan to develop the infrastructure along the Southwest border, thousands of jobs will be created to the benefit of the local community. For instance, in El Paso, TX alone, even at only the GM level, over 2,200 jobs will be created (Detention Facility – 1,000, ORR Shelter – 666, Two Adjacent Facilities – 666). This doesn't even factor in the additional jobs that will be created as a result of the transportation contract.

Strengthen the economy for border cities

Local, State and Federal Government pretty much set the tone of the economy. This is especially true along the United States.- Mexico border, because the border in itself creates economic conditions that the government entities contribute in shaping. Moreover, although the policy makers of the federal government are located in Washington, DC, they often make policy decisions that impact the border cities. As a result, the border city citizens and businesses are left at the mercy of these policy makers to either prosper economically or not.

In creating new jobs, as a result of developing the infrastructure along the Southwest border, the thousands of additional jobs and salaries will lead to additional monies spent within the local communities. And through this ripple effect of more spending at the local businesses, this should help the border cities strengthen their local economy. It might even lead to the creation of other local businesses.

Reduce the possibility of spreading infectious diseases

As stated previously, in a study conducted by the Henry M Jackson School of International Studies, they calculated that ICE Air Operations flew approximately 1.73 million detainees on nearly 15,000 flight missions in an eight-year span (October 1, 2010 to December 5, 2018). In addition, they found that 28.78% of the flights involved internal transfers, whereby approximately 500,000 detainees were being moved from one location to another within the United States.

The Henry M Jackson School of International Studites also found that the participating airports within the United States included ICE Air's five main hubs (Mesa, AZ; Brownsville, TX; Miami, FL; San Antonio, TX; and Alexandria, LA); as well as 83 other airports scattered across the country, some in "sanctuary" jurisdictions like Seattle, WA; Oakland, CA; or Minneapolis, MN. In all, during the eight-year span, ICE Air operations involved 88 airports in the United States.

Besides taking notice that internal transfer flights are very expensive, which ICE Air pays, on average, $8,577 per flight hour for charter flights regardless of the number of passengers on the plane, Congress and the Department need to take notice that there is a possibility that these internal transfer flights might serve as a mechanism to heighten the possibility of a contagious disease being spread within the United States.

Based from the study, during this eight-year span, on average, ICE Air transferred approximately 62,200 detainees from one location to another within the United States. In my experience, the vast majority of these transfers originate in locations along the Southwest border and end at locations far from the border (i.e. San Diego, CA to Atlanta, GA). Thus, if a detainee is infected, and then transferred, the contagious disease just made its way to the interior part of the United States.

To further complicate the matter, at capacity, ICE Air flights hold up to 135 detainees and are staffed by a pilot, flight attendants, security guards, and a flight nurse, as well as an ICE agent or agents. The staff normally do not reside at the origination or destination location. Also, it is a common scheduling practice for ICE Air flights to stop at multiple locations to deliver detainees at other locations between the origination and destination location so to help ICE keep all of its facilities at capacity. This is a big reason why during the eight-year span ICE involved 88 airports in the United States.

Upon taking all of this into account, it is not difficult to realize that these flights can easily contribute to spreading an infectious disease. Moreover, even if only one infected detainee boards a flight, there stands a good chance that multiple interior locations within the United States will be exposed to the virus. During a pandemic (e.g. COVID-19), this could be catastrophic.

The study did not take into account internal transfers that occurred on a daily basis via bus along the Southwest border to locations like Houston, TX; Los Angeles, CA; Phoenix, AZ; and San Antonio, TX, which is another reason why the facilities and infrastructure need to be developed along the Southwest border.

CHAPTER 7: GRANT CUSTODY AUTHORITY TO CBP

The Immigration and Nationality Act (INA), as amended, provides ICE with broad authority to detain aliens believed to be removable while awaiting a determination of whether they should be removed from the United States as well as aliens ordered removed, and mandates that ICE detain certain categories of aliens (See 8 U.S.C. §§ 1225, 1226, 1226a, 1231).

Moreover, this broad custodial authority granted to ICE as part of the INA is civil, not criminal, detention, and is not to be punitive; rather, ICE is to confine detainees for the administrative purpose of holding, processing, and preparing them for removal. This authority also allows ICE to detainee a mix of men and women from a wide variety of countries and with criminal and noncriminal backgrounds.

As I stated previously, when suggesting a merger, CBP will need to be granted custodial authority, otherwise they will not be able to assume this responsibility from ICE. Moreover, unless CBP is granted this immigration authority, they will not be able to legally detain illegal aliens who are charged with violating immigration law, have entered the United States illegally, or have been ordered to leave the country. These are the aliens that ERO currently detains while their immigration proceedings are administered and remove from the United States when ordered to do so.

In addition, this authority will allow CBP to administer a detention program that is comparable to ERO's, which uses specified appropriated congressional funds to care for the detainees taken into custody. Moreover, these dedicated funds pay for the transportation, housing, subsistence, medical care, and guard service necessary to provide safe and humane environments to the detainee population and detention staff. The responsibility begins when a detainee is brought into custody and continues until the detainee can be released into the community or removed from the United States.

Also, upon receiving this authority, instead of reinventing the wheel, it will be wise for CBP to mirror ERO's detention model for adults and its very strict 2011 performance-based national detention standards (PBNDS), which is even more tedious than the American Correctional Association's accreditation guidelines. It's also why ERO has one of the lowest rates of deaths in custody of any program within the state and federal detention system.

As proof, the Department of Justice, Office of Justice Programs, *Bureau of Justice Statistics*, found in a quick review, when tracking the national mortality rate of individuals in confinement, that the average mortality rate in state prisons was 256 deaths per 100,000 persons, and 225 for federal prisons[10]. As for ERO, in the same period, ERO averaged only 2.25 deaths per 100,000 persons. Even more amazing, although ERO has approximately 400,000 detainees go through their custody every year, they only average nine deaths per year. Meaning, state and local facilities have a death rate over 2000 percent higher than ERO's.[11]

As a result, it is imperative that Congress either amend or create a new section in the INA to provide CBP with this broad authority, and then have CBP apply ERO's 2011 PBNDS to its adult detention facilities.

CHAPTER 8: TURN TO THE PRIVATE SECTOR FOR GUIDANCE

Since the unveiling of DHS, ICE Headquarters (HQ) has traditionally turned to its HQ staff to address very complicated infrastructure issues that often are outside of their area of expertise, because the staffers usually do not have any prior experience or training in developing infrastructure. For instance, ICE HQ often turns to their officer corps and management and program analysts (MPAs) to create plans to develop infrastructures tied to detention facilities and air and ground transportation, although the officers and MPAs are not subject matter experts in these areas. In large part, this is because, prior to coming to ICE HQ, the vast majority of the officers that come to HQ have only dealt with officer related activities (e.g. administrative and criminal arrests, docket management, escorts, detainee and staff communication, etc.).   To put this in perspective, this is like FedEx or UPS directing a police officer to develop the routes for their package deliveries, or Marriott or Hilton asking an officer to review and agree on a construction plan to build a new hotel for their guests.

As a result of turning to non-subject matter experts to handle these critical duties, ICE routinely experiences shortfalls in managing its detention beds efficiently. This became obvious to the other DHS components and to our legislatures during the 2018 humanitarian crisis, because although beds became available in the various facilities from one day to another during the border crisis, ICE often took days, and sometimes up to a week, to backfill the vacant beds. Obviously, this caused a lot of frustration from the Southwest border CBP and ERO components, because during the surge, they had nowhere else to turn to for relief. In hindsight, it's obvious these delays were a result of the offices receiving inadequate air and bus transportation support during the crisis. It's also obvious that ICE's air and bus transportation operations lack the necessary structure to efficiently operate such a large-scale requirement. This is why I highly recommend that ICE start turning to a person and/or entity outside of the Agency who possesses these skillsets for advice.

I'm not pretending to be an expert in these particular areas; however, I am wise enough to know that the Department needs to improve in these areas in the event that another border crisis occurs. It's also why I highly recommend that the Department start to turn to actual subject matter experts to help them manage these transportation requirements more efficiently and stop turning to current and former officer corps employees and contractors with no proven track record in developing infrastructure and transportation support for advice. For instance, to help them operate their transportation operations more efficiently, I highly recommend that the Department seek advice from a person (retired executive) and/or entity (e.g. American Airlines, FedEx, Greyhound, United Airlines, UPS, etc.) that has a proven track record in 'successfully' managing large-scale routes efficiently in the private sector.

As for the future construction of Family Residential Centers (FRCs)[12], I believe it will be best for the Department to solicit advise on how to design the FRCs from a person or entity with extensive experience in the hotel industry. For those of us who have served with ICE, it's common knowledge amongst us that the stakeholders' major complaint with the FRCs is how they are designed, because the stakeholders believe that the layout of the facilities is far too similar to the layout of detention facilities. In my opinion, this is because ICE currently only turns to contractors (e.g. GEO, CCA, etc.) who only know how to build detention facilities to build the FRCs.

Although I am not suggesting that the Department should start building FRCs with the same design as a Hilton or Marriott hotel, I believe that a former hotel executive can offer a lot of good advice on how to make the design of the FRCs less confinement-like so that the families, especially the children, will feel less threatened to be detained in them.

CHAPTER 9: INTRODUCE A BIPARTISAN IMMIGRATION REFORM BILL

As I alluded to in the 'Introduction' of the book, Congress has failed to address the needed Immigration Reform issue for decades. As a result, anywhere from 10.5 to 14.3 million unlawfully present immigrants are residing in the United States. Of which, approximately 700,000 are currently in limbo as Deferred Action for Childhood Arrivals (DACA) applicants. Moreover, they respectively make up 3.18 to 4.33 percent of the population in the United States, and DACA recipients less than one percent. Too many for ICE to round up to deport, but far too few for one to consider a real threat to take away an appealing job from an American worker.

Congress has made several honest attempts to try to resolve the immigration issue. For instance, in 1955, as part of the reorganization of the former INS, they created the Detention and Deportation Program (D&DP), which is now referred to as the Enforcement and Removal Operations (ERO). The creation of the D&DP empowered INS to carry out the mission first articulated in the Alien and Sedition Acts of 1798, which included the earliest deportation legislation and empowered the President to order the departure from the United States of all aliens deemed dangerous. Obviously, since then, legislation has redefined the classes of aliens to be removed from the United States.

The Immigration and Nationality Act (INA) of 1952 expanded the Federal expulsion power to include a wider category of aliens. The INA listed 19 general classes of deportable aliens and provided for exclusion, at the time of application for admission, to the United States on health, criminal, moral, economic, subversive, and other grounds. The Illegal Immigration Reform and Immigrant Responsibility Act (IIRIRA) of 1996 expanded the number of crimes that made people subject to removal. It also eliminated the INS discretion to release certain aliens by requiring that virtually any non-citizen subject to removal on the basis of a criminal conviction, as well as certain categories of non-criminal aliens, be detained without bond. As a result of these acts and other legislation the INS is required to detain and remove a much larger and more diverse population. The current population requires unique facilities, procedures and management of people by risk and criminal category as well as nationality, health and all those with other special needs.

Then, on March 1, 2003, as a response to the 9/11 terrorist attacks on the United States, Congress created the Department of Homeland Security (DHS) to protect the United States from further terrorist threats through the rigorous and strict enforcement of the nation's immigration laws. ERO is one of the agencies formed as the result of the creation of DHS. Its mission is critical to the immigration enforcement process, because besides providing the interior enforcement piece, it provides the back-end support to the border agencies.

However, although all of the prior legislation received significant national attention, when they were introduced, it's safe to say that all of them still come a distant second, as far as drawing the attention of the American people, both good and bad, in comparison to President Reagan's Immigration Reform and Control Act of 1986, which he signed on November 6, 1986 in an attempt 'To humanely regain control of our borders.'

The 1986 Act received a lot of attention, and considered controversial, because many Americans were opposed to granting amnesty to nearly 3 million undocumented immigrants who only had to prove that they had been in the United States prior to Jan. 1, 1982.

Many were also opposed to the Act, because the legislation had several flaws in it. For instance, the sanctions against employers who hired undocumented immigrants have not been consistently enforced and the Act failed to include a section that would allow the 'legal' entry of low-skilled workers to handle the less desirable, labor intensive work in the United States. As a result, and because Congress failed to hold its end of the bargain, which was to put legislation in place to secure the borders, undocumented immigrants continue to illegal enter the United States to pursue these available low-income jobs.

President Reagan truly believed that this Act would help the United States get a handle on this issue. It's why many believe he went as far as saying "Future generations of Americans will be thankful for our efforts to humanely regain control of our borders and thereby preserve the value of one of the most sacred possessions of our people: American citizenship."

However, although he stated "It will remove the incentive for illegal immigration by eliminating the job opportunities which draw illegal aliens here," he realized afterwards that this would not ever come to fruition. This is likely why Republican U.S. Senate Kelli Ward said in an interview on Breitbart News' satellite radio show that "In 1986, Ronald Reagan — great president, amazing conservative, lover of liberty and of America — granted amnesty; and Ed Rollins, who is helping me with my campaign, told me that President Reagan's biggest regret as president was granting amnesty and then trusting Congress to deliver on border security. It didn't happen then, and it's not going to happen now if we do this in the wrong order."

David Bier, now an immigration policy analyst with the libertarian Cato Institute, has a different account and interpretation of why President Reagan believed his Reform Act was not successful, which is more on the opposite side of the spectrum of it failing due Congress not delivering on border security. Bier is more under the impression that President Reagan believed that his Act failed, because we refused to allow more immigrants to come. This is why he was quoted as saying "It seems that Reagan would understand that his law failed to stop illegal immigration, not because we allowed people to stay, but because we refused to allow more to come — in his farewell address, he said he wanted an America 'open to anyone with the will and heart to get here,'"

In an attempt to fulfill President Reagan's 1986 Immigration Reform and Control Act, and find a happy medium between Senator Ward and Mr. Bier's account of why President Reagan believed his Act failed, I propose that Congress revisit the 1986 Act and revise segments of the Act or create new legislation, and in the same kind hearted and humane spirit of our 132 million[13] American ancestors, when they allowed over 1 million[14] people to immigrate to the United States during World War II, and with following in mind.

Pathway to citizenship

I propose that Congress introduce a bi-partisan bill that will allow unlawfully present immigrants a pathway to citizenship. However, unlike President Reagan's Act, which allowed blanket amnesty, I propose that the bill require unlawful immigrants to 'earn' their pathway to citizenship by demonstrating they are law abiding members of society who will not commit a criminal offense.

With this being said, I think that the bill should create or modify a temporary workers visa(s) that will allow unlawfully present immigrants to remain in the United States lawfully.

Currently, temporary worker visas are for persons who want to enter the United States for employment lasting a fixed period of time, and are not considered permanent or indefinite. Each of these visas requires the prospective employer to first file a petition with U.S. Citizenship and Immigration Services (USCIS). An approved petition is required to apply for a work visa. The following chart reflects the current temporary worker visa categories.

Visa category	General description – About an individual in this category:
H-1B: Person in Specialty Occupation	To work in a specialty occupation. Requires a higher education degree or its equivalent. Includes fashion models of distinguished merit and ability and government-to-government research and development, or co-production projects administered by the Department of Defense.
H-1B1: Free Trade Agreement (FTA) Professional - Chile, Singapore	To work in a specialty occupation. Requires a post-secondary degree involving at least four years of study in the field of specialization. (Note: This is not a petition-based visa. For application procedures, please refer to the website for the U.S. Embassy in Chile or the U.S. Embassy in Singapore.)
H-2A: Temporary Agricultural Worker	For temporary or seasonal agricultural work. Limited to citizens or nationals of designated countries, with limited exceptions, if determined to be in the United States interest.
H-2B: Temporary Non-agricultural Worker	For temporary or seasonal non- agricultural work. Limited to citizens or nationals of designated countries, with limited exceptions, if determined to be in the United States interest.
H-3: Trainee or Special Education visitor	To receive training, other than graduate medical or academic, that is not available in the trainee's home country or practical training programs in the education of children with mental, physical, or emotional disabilities.
L: Intracompany Transferee	To work at a branch, parent, affiliate, or subsidiary of the current employer in a managerial or executive capacity, or in a position requiring specialized knowledge. Individual must have been employed by the same employer abroad continuously for 1 year within the three preceding years.
O: Individual with Extraordinary Ability or Achievement	For persons with extraordinary ability or achievement in the sciences, arts, education, business, athletics, or extraordinary recognized achievements in the motion picture and television fields, demonstrated by sustained national or international acclaim, to work in their field of expertise. Includes persons providing essential services in support of the above individual.
P-1: Individual or Team Athlete, or Member of an Entertainment Group	To perform at a specific athletic competition as an athlete or as a member of an entertainment group. Requires an internationally recognized level of sustained performance. Includes persons providing essential services in support of the above individual.
P-2: Artist or Entertainer (Individual or Group)	For performance under a reciprocal exchange program between an organization in the United States and an organization in another country. Includes persons providing essential services in support of the above individual.
P-3: Artist or Entertainer (Individual or Group)	To perform, teach or coach under a program that is culturally unique or a traditional ethnic, folk, cultural, musical, theatrical, or artistic performance or presentation. Includes persons providing essential services in support of the above individual.
Q-1: Participant in an International Cultural Exchange Program	For practical training and employment and for sharing of the history, culture, and traditions of your home country through participation in an international cultural exchange program.

Some temporary worker categories are limited in total number of petitions which can be approved on a yearly basis. Before an applicant can apply for a temporary worker visa at a U.S. Embassy or Consulate, a Petition for a Nonimmigrant Worker, Form I-129, must be filed on the applicant's behalf by a prospective employer and be approved by USCIS. Once the petition is approved, USCIS will send the prospective employer a Notice of Action, Form I-797.

After USCIS approves the Petition for a Nonimmigrant Worker (Form I-129), the applicant may apply for a visa.

H-2A (Temporary Agricultural Worker Visa):

The H-2A program allows U.S. employers or U.S. agents who meet specific regulatory requirements to bring foreign nationals to the United States to fill temporary agricultural jobs. A U.S. employer, a U.S. agent as described in the regulations, or an association of U.S. agricultural producers named as a joint employer must file Form I-129, Petition for a Nonimmigrant Worker, on a prospective worker's behalf.

To qualify for H-2A nonimmigrant classification, the petitioner must:

1. Offer a job that is of a temporary or seasonal nature.

2. Demonstrate that there are not enough U.S. workers who are able, willing, qualified, and available to do the temporary work.

3. Show that employing H-2A workers will not adversely affect the wages and working conditions of similarly employed U.S. workers.

4. Generally, submit a single valid temporary labor certification from the U.S. Department of Labor with the H-2A petition. (A limited exception to this requirement exists in certain "emergent

circumstances." See e.g., 8 CFR 214.2(h)(5)(x) for specific details.)

H-2A and H-2B petitions may only be approved for nationals of countries that the secretary of Homeland Security has designated, with the concurrence of the Office of the Secretary of State, as eligible to participate in the H-2 program.

The Department of Homeland Security publishes the list of H-2A and H-2B eligible countries in a Federal Register notice. Designation of eligible countries is valid for one year from publication.

Effective Jan. 19, 2020, nationals from the following countries are eligible to participate in the H-2A and H-2B program:

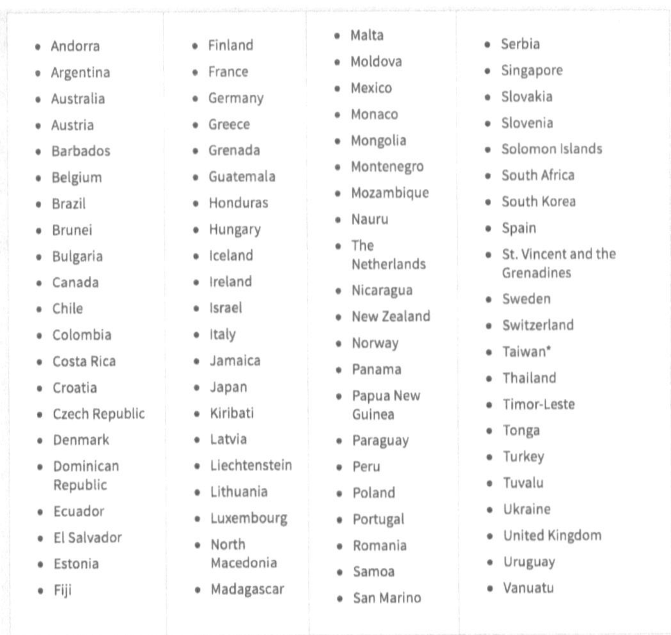

Andorra	Finland	Malta	Serbia
Argentina	France	Moldova	Singapore
Australia	Germany	Mexico	Slovakia
Austria	Greece	Monaco	Slovenia
Barbados	Grenada	Mongolia	Solomon Islands
Belgium	Guatemala	Montenegro	South Africa
Brazil	Honduras	Mozambique	South Korea
Brunei	Hungary	Nauru	Spain
Bulgaria	Iceland	The Netherlands	St. Vincent and the Grenadines
Canada	Ireland	Nicaragua	Sweden
Chile	Israel	New Zealand	Switzerland
Colombia	Italy	Norway	Taiwan*
Costa Rica	Jamaica	Panama	Thailand
Croatia	Japan	Papua New Guinea	Timor-Leste
Czech Republic	Kiribati	Paraguay	Tonga
Denmark	Latvia	Peru	Turkey
Dominican Republic	Liechtenstein	Poland	Tuvalu
Ecuador	Lithuania	Portugal	Ukraine
El Salvador	Luxembourg	Romania	United Kingdom
Estonia	North Macedonia	Samoa	Uruguay
Fiji	Madagascar	San Marino	Vanuatu

Regarding all references to "country" or "countries" in this document, it should be noted that the Taiwan Relations Act of 1979, Pub. L. No. 96-8, Section 4(b)(1), provides that "[w]henever the laws of the United States refer or relate to foreign countries, nations, states, governments, or similar entities, such terms shall include and such laws shall apply with respect to Taiwan." See 22 U.S.C. § 3303(b)(1). Accordingly, all references to "country" or "countries" in the regulations governing whether nationals of a country are eligible for H-2 program participation. See 8 CFR 214.2(h)(5)(i)(F)(1)(i) and 8 CFR 214.2(h)(6)(i)(E)(1), are read to include Taiwan. This is consistent with the United States' one-China policy, under which the United States has maintained unofficial relations with Taiwan since 1979.

Generally, USCIS may grant H-2A classification for up to the period of time authorized on the temporary labor certification. H-2A classification may be extended for qualifying employment in increments of up to 1 year each. A new, valid temporary labor certification covering the requested time must accompany each extension request. The maximum period of stay in H-2A classification is 3 years.

A person who has held H-2A nonimmigrant status for a total of 3 years must depart and remain outside the United States for an uninterrupted period of 3 months before seeking readmission as an H-2A nonimmigrant. Additionally, previous time spent in other H or L classifications counts toward total H-2A time.

Exception: Certain periods of time spent outside of the United States may "interrupt" an H-2A worker's authorized stay and not count toward the 3-year limit.

An H-2A worker's spouse and unmarried children under 21 years of age may seek admission in H-4 nonimmigrant classification. Family members are not eligible for employment in the United States while in H-4 status.

Note: On April 20, 2020, the Department of Homeland Security and USCIS published a temporary final rule to amend certain H-2A requirements to help U.S. agricultural employers avoid disruptions in lawful agricultural-related employment, protect the nation's food supply chain, and lessen impacts from the coronavirus (COVID-19) public health emergency.

Due to travel restrictions and visa processing limitations as a result of actions taken to mitigate the spread of COVID-19, as well as the possibility that some H-2A workers may become unavailable due to COVID-19 related illness, U.S. employers who have approved H-2A petitions or who will be filing H-2A petitions might not receive all of the workers requested to fill the temporary positions, and similarly, employers that currently employ H-2A workers may lose the services of workers due to COVID-19 related illness.

Under this temporary final rule, all H-2A petitioners with a valid temporary labor certification (TLC) can now start employing certain foreign workers who are currently in the United States and in valid H-2A status immediately after USCIS receives the H-2A petition, but no earlier than the start date of employment listed on the petition.

Additionally, USCIS is temporarily amending its regulations to allow H-2A workers to stay beyond the three-year maximum allowable period of stay in the United States. These temporary changes will encourage and facilitate the lawful employment of foreign temporary and seasonal agriculture workers during the COVID-19 national emergency.

The temporary final rule is effective immediately upon publication in the Federal Register. If the new petition is approved, the H-2A worker will be able to stay in the United States for a period of time not to exceed the validity period of the Temporary Labor Certification. DHS will issue a new temporary final rule in the Federal Register to amend the termination date in the event DHS determines that circumstances demonstrate a continued need for the temporary changes to the H-2A regulations.

H-2B (Temporary Non-Agricultural Worker Visa):

The H-2B program allows U.S. employers or U.S. agents who meet specific regulatory requirements to bring foreign nationals to the United States to fill temporary nonagricultural jobs. A U.S. employer, or U.S. agent as described in the regulations, must file Form I-129, Petition for a Nonimmigrant Worker, on a prospective worker's behalf.

There is a statutory numerical limit, or "cap," on the total number of aliens who may be issued an H-2B visa or otherwise granted H-2B status during a fiscal year. Currently, Congress has set the H-2B cap at 66,000 per fiscal year, with 33,000 for workers who begin employment in the first half of the fiscal year (October 1 - March 31) and 33,000 for workers who begin employment in the second half of the fiscal year (April 1 - September 30). Any unused numbers from the first half of the fiscal year will be available for employers seeking to hire H-2B workers during the second half of the fiscal year. However, unused H-2B numbers from one fiscal year do not carry over into the next.

Once the H-2B cap is reached, USCIS may only accept petitions for H-2B workers who are exempt from the H-2B cap[15].

Like the H-2A, H-2B petitions may only be approved for nationals of countries that the secretary of Homeland Security has designated, with the concurrence of the Office of the Secretary of State, as eligible to participate in the H-2B program.

Generally, USCIS may grant H-2B classification for up to the period of time authorized on the temporary labor certification. H-2B classification may be extended for qualifying employment in increments of up to 1 year each. A new, valid temporary labor certification covering the requested time must accompany each extension request. The maximum period of stay in H-2B classification is 3 years.

A person who has held H-2B nonimmigrant status for a total of 3 years must depart and remain outside the United States for an uninterrupted period of 3 months before seeking readmission as an H-2B nonimmigrant. Additionally, previous time spent in other H or L classifications counts toward total H-2B time.

Exception: Certain periods of time spent outside of the United States may "interrupt" an H-2B worker's authorized stay and not count toward the 3-year limit.

Any H-2B worker's spouse and unmarried children under 21 years of age may seek admission in H-4 nonimmigrant classification. Family members are not eligible for employment in the United States while in H-4 status.

Note: On May 14, 2020, the Department of Homeland Security published a temporary final rule to change certain H-2B requirements to help secure the U.S. food supply chain and reduce the economic impact of the coronavirus (COVID-19) public health emergency on H-2B employers.

Under this temporary final rule, an H-2B petitioner with an approved temporary labor certification can start employing H-2B workers already in the United States for positions essential to the U.S. food supply chain, immediately after USCIS receives the H-2B petition and the new attestation, but no earlier than the start date of employment listed on the petition. Additionally, DHS is temporarily amending its regulations to allow certain H-2B workers to stay beyond the three-year maximum allowable period of stay in the United States.

To take advantage of this time-limited change in regulatory requirements, the H-2B workers must be in the United States and in valid H-2B status on or after March 1, 2020. In addition, the H-2B petitioner will be required to submit, with its petition, a new Form ATT-H2B, Attestation (Confirmation) for Employers Seeking to Employ H-2B Nonimmigrant Workers Essential to the U.S. Food Chain (PDF), swearing under penalty of perjury that the H-2B worker(s) will be performing temporary nonagricultural services or labor that are essential to the U.S. food supply chain including, but not limited to:

Processing, manufacturing, and packaging of human and animal food;

Transporting human and animal food from farms or manufacturing or processing plants to distributors and end sellers; and

Selling human and animal food through a variety of sellers or retail establishments, including restaurants.

In addition to H-2B petitioners who file their petitions on or after May 14, 2020, the temporary final rule allows certain H-2B employers and U.S. agents, with pending petitions on or after that date, to request the flexibilities provided under the temporary final rule by submitting the new Form ATT-H2B attestation to the appropriate center before USCIS adjudicates their petitions.

The temporary final rule is effective immediately upon publication in the Federal Register. H-2B employers and U.S. agents can request the flexibilities authorized under the temporary final rule through Sept. 11, 2020.

Create H-2A1 and H-2B1 Visas:

In a recent study conducted by the Migration Policy Institute (MPI), the MPI found that 67 percent of the United States' undocumented immigrant population came from the Northern Triangle countries (Mexico and Central America). In addition, the study determined that 95 percent of the undocumented population either possessed a job (67 percent) or not part of the labor force (28 percent). Meaning, only 5 percent of them were unemployed, which solidifies the notion that the sole purpose of the vast majority of the unlawfully present immigrants in coming the United States is to seek employment (not to commit a crime). The MPI study also found that they mostly seek labor-intensive jobs (e.g. food services, construction, manufacturing, waste management services, etc.) that are usually not sought by the American workforce (Please refer to the following chart for additional details).

Demographics	Estimate	% of Total
Unauthorized Population	11,300,000	100%
Top Countries of Birth		
Mexico	5,944,000	53%
El Salvador	655,000	6%
Guatemala	525,000	5%
China	362,000	3%
Honduras	355,000	3%
Regions of Birth		
Mexico and Central America	7,593,000	67%
Caribbean	351,000	3%
South America	685,000	6%
Europe/Canada/Oceania	579,000	5%
Asia	1,774,000	16%
Africa	318,000	3%
Years of U.S. Residence		
Less than 5	2,009,000	18%
5 to 9	2,246,000	20%
10 to 14	2,722,000	24%
15 to 19	1,936,000	17%
20 or more	2,387,000	21%

Workforce	Estimate	% of Total
Labor Force Participation		
Civilian population ages 16 and older	10,491,000	100%
Employed	7,003,000	67%
Unemployed	546,000	5%
Not in the labor force	2,942,000	28%
Top Industries of Employment		
Civilian employed population ages 16 and older	7,003,000	100%
Accommodation and food services, arts, entertainment, and recreation	1,364,000	19%
Construction	1,194,000	17%
Professional, scientific, management, administrative, and waste management services	1,069,000	15%
Manufacturing	939,000	13%
Retail trade	737,000	11%
Economics	Estimate	% of Total
Family Income		
Below 50% of the poverty level	1,351,000	12%
50-99% of the poverty level	1,828,000	16%
100-149% of the poverty level	1,868,000	17%
150-199% of the poverty level	1,682,000	15%
At or above 200% of the poverty level	4,570,000	40%

Source: Migration Policy Institute (MPI) analysis of U.S. Census Bureau data from the pooled 2012-16 American Community Survey (ACS) and the 2008 Survey of Income and Program Participation (SIPP), drawing on a methodology developed in consultation with James Bachmeier of Temple University and Jennifer Van Hook of The Pennsylvania State University, Population Research Institute.

Keeping this in mind, it's time for Congress to agree in allowing a large segment of the unlawfully present population to remain in the United States. I propose that they allow the population from the Northern Triangle countries to remain since they make up 67 percent of the unlawfully present population, and as I mentioned previously, are mostly only seeking jobs that most Americans are not pursuing.

I believe that Congress can accomplish this if they are willing to create additional temporary worker visas that will augment the H-2A and H-2B categories. Furthermore, I believe that Congress can accomplish this by creating the H-2A1 and H-2B1 visa categories.

The H-2A1 visa category (Norther Triangle Temporary Agricultural Worker Visa) and H-2B1 (Northern Triangle Temporary Non-Agricultural Worker Visa) can serve to allow the Northern Triangle undocumented population to remain in the United States, I'm thinking as long as they are required to meet certain conditions and requirements. For instance:

1. Have not committed or suspected of committing a crime that constitute a Priority 1 (threats to national security, border security, and public safety) or Priority 2 (misdemeanants offenses) violation under President Obama's Civil Immigration Enforcement Priorities (See next section for further information).

2. Are a citizen of Mexico, El Salvador, Guatemala or Honduras.

3. Are currently unlawfully present in the United States.

4. Are currently employed in an occupation that qualifies under the H-2A or H-2B visa criteria, or are a family member who qualifies under the H-4 visa requirements.

5. Have an employer who will submit a petition on the H-2A1 or H-2B1 applicant's behalf and meet the H-2A or H-2B qualifications to submit a petition.

Upon satisfying the aforementioned conditions and requirements, the qualifying applicants should be allowed to receive either the H-2A1 or H-2B1 visa. However, unlike the H-2A or H-2B process, the applicant should not be required to leave the country to obtain the visa, but instead, should be allowed to obtain the visa through USCIS.

In addition, in an attempt to benefit the tax payers and voters in the United States, the H-2A1 and H-2B1 applicants should be required to pay a $1,000 fine as a penalty for residing in the United States unlawfully.

If my calculations are correct, based on MPI's analysis, this could draw in almost $4.5 billion[16] to the United States government, which is monies the government can put to good use as a result of the 2020 COVID-19 pandemic. And, this is besides the possible trillion of dollars that a range of economic researchers estimate that these workers would boost the U.S. GDP and the estimated additional hundred billion dollars in state and federal tax revenue from them currently; because, the research has shown that immigrants living and working in the United States without authorization are earning far less than their potential, paying much less in taxes, and contributing significantly less to the U.S. economy than they would if they were given the opportunity to gain legal status.

Furthermore, besides allowing the qualifying population to remain in the United States on a temporary basis, the bi-partisan legislation should allow for some form of pathway to citizenship. This can be accomplished through a process that requires the H-2A1, H-2B1 and respective H-4 visa holders to renew their visas every three years (without having to leave the country), and then after 10 years, if they have not committed a Priority 1 or 2 related crime, to be able to apply for permanent residency.

Apart from drawing in more revenue to the U.S. economy and government, granting legal status and eventual citizenship to the unlawfully present population from the Northern Triangle countries can help booster national security and public safety; because, it will motivate millions of undocumented immigrants to come forward and out of hiding.   In doing so, it will give the government a better account of who is residing in the United States so the law enforcement community can focus more on those who are committing crimes and endangering our local communities. In addition, it will help the immigrant community feel more at ease in reporting crimes within their communities, because they will no longer need to feel anxious about being arrested due to their unlawful immigrant status.   It also adds an extra-incentive for them to not commit a criminal offense.

Only Target Criminal Aliens

ICE's website discloses that "In Fiscal Year (FY) 2019, ICE's Enforcement and Removal Operations (ERO) officers arrested approximately 143,000 aliens and removed more than 267,000 – which is an increase in removals from the prior year. While the numbers of individuals apprehended or found inadmissible at the border nationwide increased 68% over the previous fiscal year, the total number of aliens arrested by ICE dropped by nearly 10% compared to FY 2018. Nevertheless, more than 86% of those arrested by ICE had criminal convictions or pending charges."

As suggested above, ICE does a respectable job at identifying, arresting and removing criminal aliens (i.e. 86% arrested in FY 2018 had criminal convictions or pending charges).   However,

I think that ICE can significantly improve its image by not only changing its name, but by also only using its resources to target criminal aliens. Besides it being better received by the general public, targeting criminal aliens is more in line with the Department's mission in providing public safety and national security, which is why ICE was placed within DHS.

Moreover, to simplify enforcement activities for the officers, I propose that ICE only use its resources to target aliens who fall within President Obama's priority 1 and 2 civil immigration enforcement priorities, which are:

Priority 1 (Aliens who pose a danger to national security or risk to public safety):

aliens engaged in or suspected of terrorism or espionage, or who otherwise pose a danger to national security;

aliens apprehended at the border or ports of entry while attempting to unlawfully enter the United States (transfer priority to CBP);

aliens convicted of an offense for which an element was active participation in a criminal street gang, as defined in 18 U.S.C. 521(a), or aliens not younger than 16 years of age who intentionally participated in an organized criminal gang to further the illegal activity of the gang;

aliens convicted of an offense classified as a felony in the convicting jurisdiction, other than a state or local offense for which an essential element was the alien's immigration status; and

aliens convicted of an "aggravated felony," as that term is defined in section 101(a)(43) of the Immigration and Nationality Act at the time of the conviction.

Priority 2 *(misdemeanants and new immigration violators):*

Aliens described in this priority, who are also not described in Priority 1, represent the second-highest priority for apprehension and removal. Resources should be dedicated accordingly to the removal of the following:

aliens convicted of three or more misdemeanor offenses, other than minor traffic offenses or state or local offenses for which an essential element was the alien's immigration status, provided the offenses arise out of three separate incidents;

aliens convicted of a "significant misdemeanor," which for these purposes is an offense of domestic violence; 1 sexual abuse or exploitation; burglary; unlawful possession or use of a firearm; drug distribution or trafficking; or driving under the influence; or if not an offense listed above, one for which the individual was sentenced to time in custody of 90 days or more (the sentence must involve time to be served in custody, and does not include a suspended sentence).

Remove criminal aliens from the United States under Section 238(b) authority

Section 238(b) of the Immigration and Nationality Act (INA) contains an administrative removal procedure for 'non-lawful' permanent resident aliens (LPRs) who are deportable due to a conviction for an aggravated felony. The removal procedure in 238(b) is a form of summary removal and as such, unless the alien either rebuts the charges or establishes eligibility for withholding of removal, will not be entitled to a hearing before a judge.

In order to be subject to administrative removal pursuant to section 238(b), an alien must:

Have been convicted of a crime that renders him or her deportable under section 237(a)(2)(A)(iii) of the INA (relating to aggravated felonies in immigration law);

Not be admitted into the United States as an LPR at the time removal proceedings commence [however, aliens admitted only as conditional permanent residents are subject to section 238(b)].

With respect to "aggravated felonies," it is important to remember that the statute refers to an "aggravated felony" in immigration law and not an "aggravated felony" pursuant to state law. Thus, it is possible that a conviction that may not be for an "aggravated felony" under the laws of the state where it was adjudicated may be an "aggravated felony" in the immigration context. The list of aggravated felonies in immigration law is found in section 101(a)(43) of the INA.

Pursuant to section 238(c) of the INA, conviction of an aggravated felony carries with it a presumption of deportability.

However, pursuant to section 238(b)(3) of the INA, an alien who is issued a Form I-851 (Notice of Intent to Issue a Final Administrative Removal Order) may not be removed until 14 calendar days have elapsed from the date that the order was issued. Under section 238(b)(4), the alien must be provided with reasonable notice of the charges of removability and with an opportunity, at no expense to the government, to consult with counsel. Furthermore, the alien must be provided with a reasonable opportunity to inspect all of the evidence and endeavor to rebut the charges. In the event that the alien provides compelling evidence to rebut the charges, the officer handling the case may issue a request for more evidence, place the alien in regular removal proceedings, or rescind the charges entirely [8 C.F.R. 238.1(d)(2)(ii)]. Therefore, due process is still intact.

In addition, there are multiple grounds under which administrative removal for an aggravated felony conviction may be contested. If the alien requests to see the findings in order to respond, he or she will have 10 calendar days from the service of the Form I-851 to respond if the I-851 is delivered in person, and 13 calendar days if the I-851 is delivered by mail.

The alien may also request withholding of removal on account of a fear of persecution or torture in his or her home country. If the alien requests withholding of removal, he or she will be granted an interview with an asylum officer upon issuance of a final order of removal for a reasonable fear determination [8 C.F.R. 238.1(f)(3)]. If a reasonable fear is established, withholding of removal may be granted. By treaty, the United States may not return an alien to a country where the alien faces a high likelihood of torture by a government official. However, it is important to note that a conviction for an aggravated felony may constitute a mandatory bar to asylum.

In an attempt to reduce the time criminal aliens are in immigration proceedings and tying up the courts, I believe that it is imperative that 'All' Priority 1 and 2 non-LPR criminal aliens (noted above) be removable under Section 238(b). As stated above, they will still be entitled to due process. The change will only speed up the removal process so that they will no longer remain in the United States to pose a threat to public safety or national security. The change will also save tax dollars, because it will reduce the time that the criminal aliens are in custody.

Target aliens with pending criminal charges and place into immigration proceedings

In stroke with the proposal to only target criminal aliens, it will also be prudent for the new Agency to also target non-LPR aliens with pending Priority 1 and 2 criminal charges. However, unlike the convicted criminal cases that qualify for removal under Section 238(b) authority, upon their arrest, it will be better to place the aliens with the pending charges into custody and then into immigration proceedings; unless, they have a prior order of removal that the Agency can reinstate (alien illegally reentered the United States after deportation or removal). Otherwise, without the conviction, one could make a legal argument that they were not afforded their due process.

In addition, it will be prudent for EOIR to create a specialized docket for the cases with pending charges so their cases can be heard in a timely manner; because, the removal of these aliens should be prioritized unless they qualify for asylum or another form of relief under our laws, or unless, in the judgment of an ICE Field Office Director, CBP Sector Chief or CBP Director of Field Operations, there are compelling and exceptional factors that clearly indicate the alien is not a threat to national security, border security, or public safety and should not therefore be an enforcement priority.

But, without the noted exceptions, the qualifying removal cases need to be removed from the United States as soon as possible, because they stand a better chance of being released from custody, thus offering them another opportunity to cause harm to others within our communities, if they remain in custody for an extended period of time.

Enroll collateral non-criminal arrests into ATD

In step with Chapter 1/Expand the Use of ATD Program, when encountered, unlawfully present non-criminal immigrant aliens (with no pending criminal charges) should be enrolled into the ATD program. Moreover, although it will be highly controversial, the Agency should cease to target these individuals for arrests, except as mentioned in the previous section, they have pending priority 1 or 2 criminal charges.

Instead, the encountered unlawfully present non-criminal immigrant aliens should be treated as follows:

1. In the event they do not have a final order of removal from an Immigration Judge (IJ), they should be served with a Notice to Appear (NTA) to go before an IJ, and then released from custody on the ATD program. They should continue to be enrolled in ATD until their immigration proceedings are completed; unless, there are compelling factors that prevent the Agency from placing them in the program (e.g. alien is a minor). In the instances that the Agency is not able to enroll somebody into ATD, the Agency should revert to using the traditional non-detained reporting method (Have the person report to the office in-person periodically). In addition, the Agency should continue to exercise prosecutorial discretion[17] on a case by case basis.

2. The encountered aliens who have received a final order of

removal from an IJ also be enrolled into the ATD or continue to be enrolled in the program (enrolled as part of bullet 1). However, they should be placed in the strictest ATD program (e.g. strict reporting requirements, unannounced visits by the ATD contractor to the enrollee's home, etc.). They should continue to remain in ATD while arrangements are made (e.g. obtain the necessary travel document, plane ticket, etc.) to remove them to their home country. On the day of the scheduled removal, arrangements should be made to report to the nearest Agency office. They will then be removed from the ATD program and taken to the airport to board the scheduled removal flight. And, as before, the Agency can choose to exercise prosecutorial discretion on a case by case basis or approve a deferred action [18] or stay of removal request[19].

3. For those aliens who have received a final order of removal and fail to report on the date of the scheduled removal flight, the Agency should take them into custody the next time they are encountered, but only as a collateral arrest. Meaning, the Agency should arrest them only when they are 'incidentally' encountered while targeting a criminal alien or during a worksite enforcement operation[20].

As I alluded to before, I understand that my proposal to not take unlawfully present non-criminal aliens into custody is a very controversial recommendation. However, despite this, this change is truly needed and long overdue. Keep in mind, in criminal law, police officers often decline to arrest people for minor offenses (like jaywalking and even minor drug possession). Moreover, when police officers enforce the law for minor traffic offenses, they normally issue either a warning or traffic ticket/

fine, and they usually do not arrest somebody; unless, the traffic offense is egregious or the person has an outstanding warrant. I am proposing that the U.S. government start enforcing immigration law in a similar fashion. There are those that will be at odds with doing this, but it can be done.

Also, keep in mind that other countries already have chosen to amend their laws to make comparable changes to their immigration laws. For instance, in July 2008, the Government of Australia announced the end of mandatory detention in Australia, unless the asylum seeker was deemed to pose a risk to the wider community, such as those who have repeatedly breached their visa conditions or those who have security or health risks. The United States only needs to follow suit.

In doing so, besides resulting into a significant cost savings to the government (See Cost Savings in Chapter 1/Expand the Use of the Alternatives to Detention (ATD) Program), this change can significantly improve the image of the Agency; because, the general public, legislators, media, and non-governmental organizations will then be hard pressed to convince mainstream America that the Agency is terrorizing immigrant communities, picking up non-criminal aliens. The statistics will speak for themselves.

The change should also help the Agency to improve its employee morale, because the officers and staff will be able to take more pride in their work in arresting criminals instead of unlawfully present families (which includes children) and workers.

The Agency will also then be able to dedicate its resources accordingly and more easily to target criminal aliens, which will make it easier for the Agency's stakeholders, including Congress, to understand and, hopefully, appreciate the Agency's mission.

CHAPTER 10: SUPPORT EMPLOYER SANCTIONS

lthough the 1986 Immigration Reform and Control Act (IRCA) was signed into law over 30 years ago, IRCA has never fulfilled President Reagan's hope in curtailing illegal immigration to the United States. In large part, this is because a key part of IRCA has not been enforced consistently.

Under IRCA, employers who hire illegal aliens are supposed to be subject to civil penalties of $250 to $10,000 for each such alien. In an interview with the New York Times (See Appendix A/President Signs Landmark Bill on Immigration), Representative Barney Frank, a Massachusetts Democrat, said "Mr. Reagan described this provision as "the keystone" of the Immigration Reform and

Control Act of 1986." He also said that President Reagan stated "It will remove the incentive for illegal immigration by eliminating the job opportunities which draw illegal aliens here."

Unfortunately, as a result of this provision not being enforced consistently, instead of stemming illegal immigration, it appears that IRCA has actually encouraged it, because the flow of illegal immigrants coming to the United States has continued and even increased since IRCA's inception.

Moreover, IRCA has done little to discourage employers from continuing to employ and exploit undocumented workers, thus resulting in illegal immigrants continuing to live in abysmal living conditions and in constant fear of apprehension, like fugitives. It also has placed illegal immigrants in a vulnerable position to where they must accept unsafe working conditions or cut wages. Otherwise, the employer will abruptly dismiss them with little fear of reprisal.

The exploitation of illegal immigrants should not sit well with either side of the House. As such, I highly recommend that Congress agree to collectively start supporting IRCA's provision in taking action against employers who employ unlawfully present immigrants. With the creation of the H-2A1 and H-2B1 Visas, which I recommended in Chapter 9/ Introduce a Bi-Partisan Bill that entails Comprehensive Immigration Reform, and the removal of the visa cap for these two visa categories, employers will no longer be able to use labor-shortages as a viable defense to employ undocumented workers. Furthermore, as an additional measure to curtail the flow of illegal immigrants and their subsequent exploitation, I highly recommend that

Congress either modify IRCA or introduce a new bill that imposes harsher punishments on those who continue to employ and exploit undocumented workers. For instance, I recommend imposing harsher fines, imprisonment, and a strict prohibition of interstate commerce in any goods produced or harvested by illegal immigrants.

CHAPTER 11:
TELEWORK PROGRAM

On December 9, 2010, President Obama signed the Telework Enhancement Act (PL 111-292) to increase the use of telework among eligible employees. The Act requires agencies to establish telework policies, determine eligibility for participation in telework, and notify employees of their eligibility to telework. Shortly, thereafter, DHS sent an official notification to employees of the basic telework eligibility requirements.

Then, on September 4, 2012, ICE Director John Morton sent all ICE employees another message entitled "2011 Federal Employee View Point Survey Results Focus on Work-life Balance", which encouraged ICE managers to consider creative ways that they might accommodate employees through flexible work schedules, telework arrangements, and other flexibilities that reduce stress and foster a healthy and vibrant workforce. However, although ICE Headquarters has made strides in implementing telework at the Headquarters' level, it has yet to make any significant impact within the 24 ICE/ERO Field Offices.

Thus, in the event Congress agrees to create a new Agency to replace ICE, the Department also needs to make it a priority to maximize the use of the Telework program at the inception of the new Agency. In allowing the eligible employees (e.g. support staff) to utilize telework on a regular basis, the cost savings to the government could easily carry over into the millions; because, telework has the potential to cut back on the required infrastructure, which will reduce the real estate and energy costs.

In addition, as stated in the "Telework Enhancement Act of 2010", it can "help recruit and retain our most qualified workforce possible, and increase employment opportunities for persons with disabilities, and help balance home/work life (i.e. less leave time if a person can work from home and still make a 4PM doctor appointment; less time spent commuting means an employee can start the workday fresh). An effective and robust telework program is also a vital component of our Continuity of Operations Plans and our general ability to continue to function during emergencies." For example, most Telework agreements possess an agreement clause that in the event the government is closed (weather, earthquakes, etc.) that the Telework participant will continue to perform his or her normal duties, unless designated Telework location is effected by the event that caused the government to close (i.e. no power due to a snow).

With this being said, upon entering the post COVID-19 pandemic era, it will be wise for all levels of government to consider implementing some form of Telework program.

CHAPTER 12:

DEUNIONIZE ICE ERO
DEPORTATION OFFICERS

According to Article 1 of the Professional Employees Agreement 2011:

U.S. Department of Homeland Security, U.S. Immigration and Customs Enforcement (hereinafter, ICE or the Agency) recognizes the American Federation of Government Employees, AFL-CIO (hereinafter, AFGE) as the exclusive collective bargaining representative for all professional employees of the Agency, as certified by the Federal Labor Relations Authority in Case No. WA-RP-07-0018 (June 22, 2007). Excluded from the bargaining unit are non-professional employees, management officials, supervisors, and employees described in 5 U.S.C. 7112(b)(2), (3), (4), (6) and (7).

The Agency acknowledges that AFGE has delegated authority for administration of this Agreement and for all other day-to-day representational functions to AFGE Local 511 (hereinafter, Local 511 or the Union). Accordingly, except for negotiation of this Collective Bargaining Agreement and for matters affecting the certification of the bargaining unit, the Agency will deal with Local 511 as AFGE's authorized representative for all labor relations matters, unless and until AFGE should give written notice to the Agency that its delegation of authority to the Agency that its delegation of authority to Local 511 has been amended or withdrawn.

As part of this agreement, the Union represents ICE Deportation Officers. Moreover, the officers may seek union representation, when the Agency is taking disciplinary or an adverse action against them. This often leads to significant delays before an action is taken against an officer, because an officer may grieve the pending action under grievance[21] and arbitration[22] procedures or appeal to the Merit Systems Protection Board (MSPB)[23]. Arbitration is usually invoked, when the Agency and the Union fail to resolve any grievance processed under the negotiated grievance procedure. In large part, this is why problematic officers continue to work while their case is pending, and are usually not removed from the officer position once a decision is made.

As I stated previously in Chapter 4/Permit CBP to Acquire ERO in the Southwest border, when ICE was created on March 1, 2003, the dismantling and reorganization of the former INS components should have been distributed slight differently. Moreover, I stated that ERO and HSI should not have been merged within the same Agency.

In addition to my recommendation to separate ERO and HSI, Congress should have removed the ICE Deportation Officers' right to union representation, when they removed this right from the former INS Criminal Investigators. This occurred, when the former INS Criminal Investigators were merged into the ICE Special Agent positions, which later changed to HSI Special Agents.

Although the Department has pushed to remove the union rights from the Deportation Officers on a few occasions, it has never come to fruition, because often, the administration does not have the appetite to entertain the change. However, now that 'officer abuse' incidents have made their way to the national spotlight, it should be an ideal time to make another push for this change, because the federal government can no longer afford to have a process in place that delays or prevents the removal of problematic law enforcement officers.

CHAPTER 13: VOTE RESPONSIBLY

After serving for the federal government for over 27 years, I've arrived to the conclusion that it's our U.S. House of Representatives that is the problem, because certain members currently serve as a barrier to prevent our great country from making any meaningful progress in rectifying our highly politicized issues. Moreover, I'm convinced that many of them are not overly concerned that these highly politicized issues are not going to be rectified anytime soon. Instead, because it is more convenient for them to do so, many of them are casting blame on the other party for not rectifying the issues, and then in a cowardly manner, unfairly casting blame on the agencies and officers for upholding the laws that 'Congress' enacts.

In addition, instead of showing a willingness to find a compromise/find a middle ground to resolve these highly politicized issues, some of the members go to the media so a planned out sound bite(s) can be captured and used against the other party, and the officers who took an oath to enforce the laws that 'Congress' enacts. As a result, the agencies and officers are often wrongfully caught in the middle of all of the negative, often false, rhetoric and finger pointing, and then left on a limb to fend for themselves. Then, to add insult to injury, these representatives go out of their way to cast blame on the agencies and officers by participating in rallies and protests (with media attention) aimed to place a negative light on an agency and officers sworn to uphold the laws that they create.

Obviously, this is hypocrisy at its highest level, because Congress is to blame for not changing the laws that the officers are required to enforce, not the Agencies. Nonetheless, the Agencies continue to be the recipient of the blame. This was on great display during the 2018 humanitarian crisis, when many of members were casting blame on CBP and ICE for not having the needed infrastructure to meet the demand of the overwhelming flow of families arriving to the Southwest border, but did little to help the agencies rectify the problem. And, although this is still a hot topic, they still have failed to change our immigration laws or appropriate more positions to ICE to assist CBP with the humanitarian crisis. They also failed to acknowledge that ICE did not separate families during the Southern border crisis, but on the contrary, ICE worked to reunite the families that CBP separated. In addition, the members failed to acknowledge that ICE played an instrumental role during the humanitarian crisis, because the agency work collectively with the local Non-Governmental Organizations (NGOs) along the Southwest border to make certain that thousands of families were released to a safe environment. The success of this humanitarian campaign was so monumental that one of the NGO members received El Paso's 2018 Citizen of the Year award. Nonetheless, ICE unfairly continued to only receive false and irresponsible rhetoric from many of our representatives.

I believe the tactic of casting blame on the agencies truly started raising its ugly head about 10 years ago. This is when many of the far left (overly liberal) and right (tea party types) representatives started to take office. Ever since, it appears that nothing of importance ever gets resolved. Moreover, it appears that the media affiliates are the only ones benefiting from this circus environment, because it often leads to higher viewer ratings.

On one side, you have the Democratic Party's Fab Four trying to do away with borders. On the other side, the overly conservative Republicans are wanting to deport everybody. They are also the members of Congress who regularly appear on the air to cast blame on each other or unfairly vilify an agency for doing its job. They also have a reputation of going out of their way to bully the middle of the road/moderate representatives to not agree on a middle ground solution with the other party. In my humble opinion, this is why nothing is getting done, except the finger pointing, and why no meaningful legislation to rectify decades-long issues, like Immigration Reform, has passed the House in several years.

It's time for us, the voters, to accept responsibility for creating our non-productive House, and start voting more responsibly. It's long overdue. Moreover, it's time to stop voting for the overly liberal and conservatives, just because their personality appeals to you. As a responsible adult and voter, it is our civic duty to make certain that our representatives are truly qualified to serve as our representatives. No offense intended towards any particular representative, but I do not believe that it is wise for us to continue to vote for a bartender, a celebrity with no prior government experience, and/or representatives with a track record of only disrupting progress instead of contributing to meaningful solutions and legislation.

With this being said, I believe that it will serve our communities better to vote for moderate/middle of the road democrats and republicans. In my experience, these are the representatives who are more willing to work out the issues and compromise on bi-partisan bills that stand a chance of becoming law. Otherwise, our country is going to continue to make no progress in rectifying these sensitive and highly important issues. Moreover, we are going to need to become accustomed to viewing the far left and right representatives on television on a regular basis, as if they are celebrities, while they make no meaningful progress in resolving our country's major issues; unless, we vote them out of office. Collectively, we have the power to change this.

ACKNOWLEDGEMENTS AND EXPRESSED GRATITUDE

Without the unconditional support of my lovely wife, Dorys, it's highly unlikely that I would have had such a successful federal career, and the time to have written this book. Throughout our marriage, she has always given me her full support, and made several sacrifices to help me further my career. This was on full display, when I asked her to leave El Paso, TX in the early years of our marriage. I know that she did it only out of the kindness of her heart and the genuine love that she has for me, because I also know that it was a huge sacrifice for her to leave her mother (her best friend) for the first time in her life. I also recall the time she had to care for Dorian and Darien alone, as babies, when we resided in Washington, DC for nearly four years. She had to do it alone, because I was working very long hours practically every day, including weekends and holidays. As a result, I was almost never at home. No offense intended to anybody, but I do not believe that there are many spouses, and rightfully so, that are willing to endure the many sacrifices that Dorys has made for me. Just image, shortly after making several good friends in a particular location, your spouse comes home from one day to another, and with no prior notice, tells you that you are going to need to pack your bags again, because we are transferring to another location again. Dorys did it for me on eight occasions. Yes, I am very fortunate to have such a loving and wonderful partner in my life. It's impossible for me to ever fully repay her for all the sacrifices that she has made for me and our children. It's why I will always love Dorys with all of my heart, and taking this time to express my gratitude for everything she has done for me and our family.

I also want to express my gratitude to my parents and siblings for everything that they have taught me throughout my life. My father taught me discipline, hard work, and keeping a high self-esteem. My mother taught me the importance of unconditional love, never backing down to anybody when you know you are right, and keeping your house in order. May she rest in peace. My oldest brother, Steve, taught me to be competitive and to always feel like a winner, even when I lost. My older sister, Mary Jane, taught me not to take any day for granted before she passed away at an early age. Yes, a day does not pass that I do not miss her and my mother. My closest brother, Jesse, taught our family the importance of staying together, once our mother passed away several years ago. My younger brother and sister, Chris and Stephanie, taught me to overcome adversity, which I know they are doing. My step-mother, Norma, also deserves my utmost respect and love, because she has filled in wonderfully since the passing of my mother. I especially appreciate the genuine love that she shows me and my siblings, Dorys and our children. These traits are now instilled in me for life thanks to all of them.

Thank you to my children (Jesse, Vanessa, Dorian and Darien) and my grandchildren (Jessica, Cecilia, Anastasia and Natalie) for bringing real meaning to my life, along with much happiness and unconditional love. My son-in-law (Barry) and daughter-in-law (Melanie) also deserve my gratitude, because they are fabulous spouses to my older children and parents to my grandchildren. I am very proud of all of them. I am also proud of my nieces and nephews.

I also owe my father-in-law (living) and mother-in-law (deceased), Jose Tirso and Mercedes, my utmost appreciation, respect and love, because they have always treated me as a member (more like a son) of the Gachupin family, along with my lovely sisters-in-law (Mercedes, Elvia, Lucy and Sarah) and brothers-in-law (Tito, Ernest and Jesus). I especially cherish the relationship that I had with my mother-in-law. I will always dearly miss her and her contagious smile.

My cousins in College Station and Houston, TX also deserve my gratitude, because they have always treated me more like a brother. I truly enjoy the special bond that we have with each other, as a result of my loving father and deceased uncles.

I thank my close friends from Oak Cliff, in Dallas, TX, who helped mold me as a youth into the person that I am today, especially the Alva, Breedings, Dunbar, Gomez, Vallejo and Wycliff family. I also want to thank my coaches and teachers from St. Elizabeth Elementary and Bishop Dunne High School for providing me with an excellent education and guidance. I would be remiss not to give special notoriety to Coach Ron Monday (St. Elizabeth Football Coach), Wayne Roeder (Bishop Dunne Football Coach) and Paul Woods (Bishop Dunne Football Coach) for the numerous young men and women that they molded into productive members of our communities across the United States. We all owe you a lot of gratitude.

UTD also helped me along the way. If it wasn't for the degree that I obtained from UTD, it's highly unlikely that I would have been able to jumpstart my federal law enforcement career. For that, I owe my alma mater my utmost respect and appreciation. GO COMETS!

I also owe a lot of gratitude to Most Reverend Bishop Mark J. Seitz and the Catholic Diocese of El Paso, because if it was not for their willingness to seek volunteers during the 2018 Southern border crises, when over 100 hundred thousand immigrant families arrived to El Paso, I would be very reluctant to say that we would have been able to find an adequate number of safe shelters to place the families. Ruben Garcia of the Annunciation House and City of El Paso and Emergency Manager Coordinator Jorge Rodriguez also played instrumental roles during the crisis. Ruben coordinated the placement of the families at the various shelters in El Paso, TX; Las Cruces, NM; and Albuquerque, NM. Jorge provided additional support within the City of El Paso, when bed space was scarce at the shelters. Working collectively, we managed to successfully overcome the significant surge of families.

Since the day that I first reported to El Paso to start my federal law enforcement career, Jesus Placencia was willing to take me under his wing to guide me in the right direction. He taught me the importance of enforcing the law in a dignified manner by treating others with dignity and respect. I did my best to follow his philosophy throughout my entire federal career. He continues to be one of my spiritual advisors. I can never repay him enough for all that he did to help me with my career.

I also had the good fortune of working for some fantastic leaders who taught me a lot. While in headquarters, I served directly under Tom Homan before I returned to the field. I truly enjoyed his sense of humor, and admired his great work ethic and willingness to defend the agency and the men and women who enforce the law. Sean Gallagher and Mike Rozos also come to mind, when I think of individuals who led people the right way. Mike was another leader willing to defend the troops. Sean Gallagher was the most well-rounded leader of all. He pretty much excelled at everything regarding leading people. This is why the vast majority of his employees admired him. It's also why it comes to no surprise to all of us who know him well that he was nominated as one of the 'Top 500 CEO's' in Atlanta, GA on more than one occasion. I truly learned a lot from them. Sean, thank you! It was truly a pleasure to work with you.

Thanks also to Adrian M, Adrian R, Al H, Al W, Albert B, Albert C, Alfie O, Altagracia M, Amy D, Andrea K, Andrew D, Angel D, Ann S, Ariek S, Arnie G, Art P, Bill J, Bill M, Bob A, Brian A, Brian V, Bruce T, Carey D, Carlos G (deceased), Carlos R, Carlos T, Carmen G, Chris C, Chris M, Chris S, Chris W, Christina A, Christine C, Calvin J, Clay T, Conrad A, Cori W, Cynthia G, Dan J, Dan W, Daniel S, Darius R, Dave J, David A, David P, David T, Deanne D, Debra G (deceased), Don G, Edgar M, Edly V, Elias E, Eric C, Erik C, Frances J, Frank R, Fred H, Gary G, George S, Gilbert A, Gilbert C, Gilbert X R, Gloria C, Gloria M, Henry A, Jaime D, JD T, Kristen S, Harvey S, Hector G, Hilario L, Ilene F, Jace C, Jack S, Jaime A, Jaime P, Jarvis M, Javier G, Jeff S, Jennifer R, Jerry O, Jesus L, Jim M, Joe W, Joedie S, Joanna S,

John F (AKA: Fab), Jose B, Jose C, Jose T, Juan S (deceased), Julie C, Jon G, Karen T, Kevin T, Kim B, Kirsti E, Lana S, Lasal A, Laura W-H, Leticia H, Leticia Z, Luis G, Lupe F, Maggie L, Marc R, Maria C, Mario R, Mark H, Marlen P, Marshall V, Martha S, Mary D, Michael J P, Mike D, Mike G, Mike I, Mike K, Mike M, Mike P, Norina C, Priscilla V, Ovidio D, Patrick D, Phil D, Rachel V, Rafael R, Raul C, Ray C, Ray P, Ray R, Ray S, Reggie S, Ricardo W, Richard R, Robert K W, Robert S, Ron M, Ron W, Roxanne D, Roy P, Russ H, Sam C, Sandra M, Scott L, Scott M, Sean E, Sean V, Shanell C, Simona F, Sirce O, Susana T, Sylvestre O, Tae J, Talia S, Teofilo L (deceased), Terry T, Thomas B, Tom H, Walter W, Wendell J, William J, Yvonne E, and all of the other friends and colleagues that I met throughout my federal career. All of you rock!

Thank you to all of the law enforcement officers, especially my cousin Pete Sifuentez (Helicopter Pilot for Houston PD) and my friends in the Dallas PD, and our military personnel across the nation and abroad for all of the personal sacrifices that you and your family make to keep our great country safe. It's because of all of you that we can continue to sleep well at night. May God bless and protect all of you and your family.

And Finally, I'd like to thank the men and women who served or are serving the Former INS or ICE. Although your role in protecting our great country is often underappreciated and/or scrutinized as a result of some of the politicians and media affiliates unfairly depicting you as villains, it does not mean that your work is not invaluable. Without your continual contributions, which result in the removal of over 100 thousand criminals to their home country every year, more criminals (from other countries) would be roaming our streets causing harm to innocent people within our communities, including immigrant communities. With this being said, please continue to fight the great fight. It is important for our public safety and national security. I thank God for blessing me with such humble and dedicated friends and colleagues. It truly was an honor to serve with all of you.

Joe Sifuentez as a young Former INS Immigration Inspector in 1994.

Joe Sifuentez (ICE Deputy Field Office Director) with DOJ Deputy Attorney General Rod Rosenstein during a town hall meeting in Georgia.

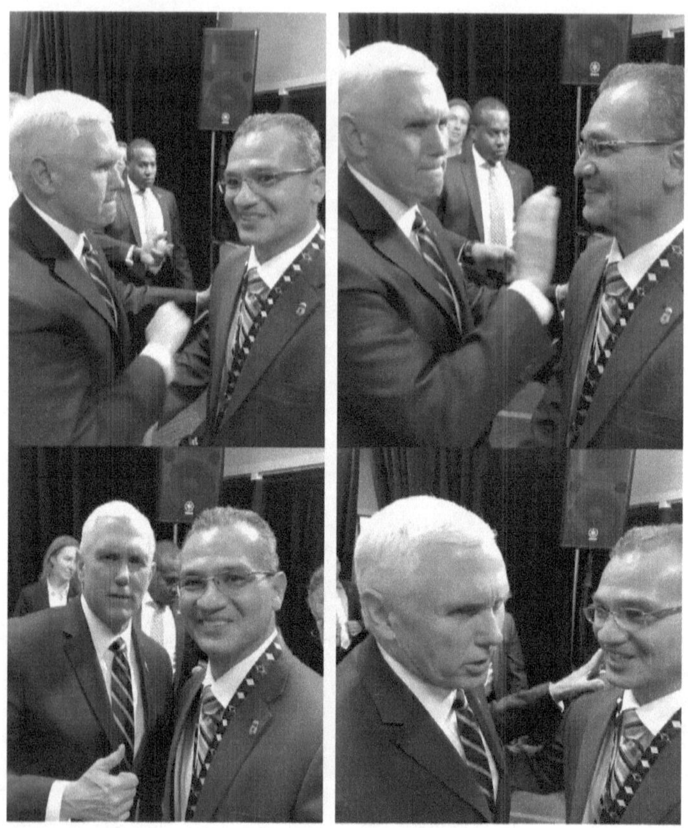

Joe Sifuentez (ICE Deputy Field Office Director) with Vice President Mike Pence during a news conference in Atlanta, Georgia.

Joe and Dora celebrating his birthday and retirement.

Joe and Dora's wedding day. Joe considers this to be the greatest day of his life, because he was able to marry the love of his life.

Photos of Joe and his children, daughter-in-law and son-in-law. He considers each of them to be a gift from God.

Joe's beautiful granddaughters. Each has their own unique personality. They all bring a lot of joy, laughter and love to Joe's life.

Joe and his loving parents, step-mother and siblings. Joe knows he is very blessed to be a member of such a loving and colorful family.

Photos of the family gatherings (Sifuentez and Gachupin). They are always filled with a lot of love and laughter.

APPENDIX A: PRESIDENT SIGNS LANDMARK BILL ON IMMIGRATION

PRESIDENT SIGNS LANDMARK BILL ON IMMIGRATION

By Robert Pear, Special to the New York Times

Nov. 7, 1986

President Reagan today signed a landmark immigration bill that prohibits employers from hiring illegal aliens and offers legal status to many illegal aliens already in the United States.

In a brief ceremony in the Roosevelt Room of the White House, surrounded by Administration officials and members of Congress who were instrumental in passing the legislation, Mr. Reagan hailed the bill as "the most comprehensive reform of our immigration laws since 1952."

"Future generations of Americans will be thankful for our efforts to humanely regain control of our borders and thereby preserve the value of one of the most sacred possessions of our people, American citizenship," the President added. Reagan Has Some Reservations

Mr. Reagan issued an unusually detailed four-page statement listing his reservations about parts of the bill and his interpretation of key provisions, including one that outlaws job discrimination against legal aliens. He said he understood this provision to require proof that the employer had a "discriminatory intent."

The author of this section, Representative Barney Frank, a Massachusetts Democrat, said in an interview that Mr. Reagan's interpretation was "intellectually dishonest, mean-spirited" and incorrect. "A pattern or practice of discriminatory activity would violate the law even if you cannot prove an intent to discriminate," Mr. Frank said. Under the new law, employers who hire illegal aliens will be subject to civil penalties of $250 to $10,000 for each such alien. Mr. Reagan described this provision as "the keystone" of the Immigration Reform and Control Act of 1986. "It will remove the incentive for illegal immigration by eliminating the job opportunities which draw illegal aliens here," he said.

The new law offers legal status, or amnesty, to aliens who can show that they entered the United States before Jan. 1, 1982, and have resided here continuously "in an unlawful status" since then. Aliens, such as foreign students or tourists, would generally be ineligible for the amnesty if they were in the United States legally for any portion of the time after Jan. 1, 1982.

Duane Austin, spokesman for the Immigration and Naturalization Service, said the agency would start accepting applications from illegal aliens next May. It will set up 90 to 100 offices around the country to handle such applications, he said. 'Headed Into Uncharted Waters'

Representative Charles E. Schumer, a Brooklyn Democrat who emerged as one of the bill's staunchest supporters in Congress, said: "The bill is a gamble, a riverboat gamble. There is no guarantee that employer sanctions will work or that amnesty will work. We are headed into uncharted waters."

However, Mr. Schumer and others said the current situation was unacceptable. The Government caught 1.8 million illegal aliens in the fiscal year ended Sept. 30, an increase of about 30 percent from the previous year. For every alien who is caught, officials say, several enter undetected.

There is no way to know how many illegal aliens are in the United States, how many are eligible for legal status or how many will apply. The Census Bureau estimates that there are three million to five million illegal aliens now in the country, but members of Congress often use higher estimates. Bill Seen as 'Humane Approach'

Senator Alan K. Simpson, a Wyoming Republican who was the chief sponsor of the bill in the Senate, expressed confidence that most employers would comply voluntarily. "I don't know what the impact will be," he said, "but this is the humane approach to immigration reform."

He and other lawmakers said they would closely monitor how the law was carried out by the immigration service and other Federal agencies. A coalition of national groups said they, too, would monitor enforcement. The coalition includes the American Immigration Lawyers Association, the National Council of La Raza, the Mexican American Legal Defense and Educational Fund, the American Civil Liberties Union and the United States Catholic Conference.

With the President's signing of the bill shortly after 10 A.M. today, it became unlawful for employers to hire illegal aliens. But the law says no penalties may be imposed for six months. In this time, the Justice Department will "disseminate forms and information to employers," as the law says.

Legislators in Mexico have said the new law will not stop illegal immigration and could endanger relations between their country and the United States. But Mr. Reagan said today that illegal immigration should not be seen as "a problem between the United States and its neighbors," adding, "Our objective is only to establish a reasonable, fair, orderly and secure system of immigration into this country and not to discriminate in any way against particular nations or people."

The major components of the bill, employer sanctions and amnesty, were proposed by President Carter in 1977 and again by Mr. Reagan in 1981. Similar bills were passed by the Senate in 1982 and 1983, but died amid political wrangling and well-organized lobbying by Hispanic groups, farm organizations and business groups. Compromise on Farm Workers

Mr. Schumer broke a deadlock over the bill this year when he negotiated a compromise to assure farmers a steady supply of foreign workers while protecting the workers' rights. The final version of the bill was approved last month in the House of Representatives by a vote of 238 to 173, and in the Senate by a vote of 63 to 24.

When the application period begins next May, illegal aliens will have one year in which to seek legal status. They would first become lawful temporary residents. After 18 months in that status, they could become permanent residents if they demonstrated a "minimal understanding" of the English language and some knowledge of the history and government of the United States.

After five years as permanent residents, aliens may apply for United States citizenship.

The new law also includes these provisions:

* An employer who shows a "pattern or practice" of hiring illegal aliens would be subject to criminal penalties, up to a $3,000 fine and six months' imprisonment.

* For five years after gaining legal status, aliens would be ineligible for welfare, food stamps and most other Federal benefits. There would be some exceptions for the aged, blind and disabled and for pregnant women.

* The Federal Government will set aside $1 billion a year to reimburse state governments for the costs of providing public assistance, health care and education to illegal aliens who gain legal status.

Congress envisions a 50 percent increase in Border Patrol personnel, who now number 3,687. But there is no guarantee that Congress will provide money for the increase.

APPENDIX B: ICE PREMIUM PAY GUIDE: AUO

Introduction:

AUO is an alternative system for the management and compensation of *"irregular and occasional"* overtime. It is designed to address the unique challenges related to positions whose duties require a significant amount of "administratively uncontrollable" overtime. Once a position is certified for AUO, AUO compensates all *"irregular or occasional overtime"* hours with an "annual premium payment," which can vary between 10 and 25 percent. *"Regularly scheduled"* overtime hours continue to be compensated with FEPA overtime ("45 Act/Title 5 overtime").

AUO provides for some trade-offs for employees and employers. While AUO-certified employees are given a significant degree of discretion in "self-initiating" overtime, they see decreased compensation for *"irregular or occasional"* overtime in certain circumstances, as compared to FEPA overtime. However, AUO-certified employees see comparably greater compensation in other circumstances, through various provisions set forth in the governing federal regulations where payment is continued but no overtime is performed. AUO is also considered with respect to calculating retirement payments.

While AUO provides significant discretion to self-initiate overtime work, that discretion is limited by the controlling regulations and must be used consistent with applicable policies, and it does not supersede supervisory instructions, including the instruction to cease performing work.

Statutory & Regulatory Authorities:

5 U.S.C. §§ 5545 & 5548; 5 CFR Part 550, Sections 101-107, 151-154, 161-164.

Rules:

The management of AUO involves three key determinations:

1. Whether an employee is *eligible* for and may be *certified* for AUO;

2. If an employee can be AUO certified, what *rate* he or she should receive; and

3. What hours of work qualify for *payment* with the AUO premium.

Certification for AUO

1. An employee may be certified for AUO if:

   a. The employee is in a position that has been determined by the Agency (at ICE, the Human Capital Officer) to be *eligible* for AUO because the duties typical to the position, as described in the position description, meet the standard set forth in 5 CFR § 550.151, in that "the hours of duty cannot be controlled administratively," and require "substantial amounts of irregular or occasional overtime work, with the employee generally being responsible for recognizing, without supervision, circumstances that require the employee to remain on duty;" and

   b. The duties of the specific employee (or "individual position") meet all of the requirements set forth in 5 CFR § 550.153, namely:

      i. The responsibility to continue on duty after the end of the workday or resuming

      ii. duty in accordance with *"irregular"* plans, as dictated by operational circumstances, is a definite, official, and special requirement inherent in employee's duties, such that failure to continue or resume working would constitute negligence or dereliction of duty, as opposed to the continuation or resumption of work being merely desirable for the employee or agency;

iii. The requirement for the *"irregular or occasional"* overtime work is not based solely on either clear-cut instances such as staying on duty until relief arrives or periodic requirements to perform call-back overtime work;

iv. The requirement for the *"irregular or occasional"* overtime work is based on work where the employee does not have discretion as to when or where the work may be performed (e.g., the requirement is not based on work where an employee has the option of taking work home or doing it at the office, or where an employee has the latitude to choose to start work later in the morning and continue working later at night);

v. The employee is expected to be required to continually work an average of at least three hours of *"irregular or occasional"* overtime work per week, generally with more than one instance of such work per week; and

vi. There is a definite basis for anticipating that the above requirements for *"irregular or occasional"* overtime work will continue throughout the period for which the particular AUO certification is valid.

2. ICE has an obligation to periodically review an employee's AUO certification for an employee to determine whether its continuation is appropriate, and, if so, to what is the appropriate AUO rate.

3. ICE must cease paying the AUO premium when an employee's duties no longer meet the qualifications for AUO (*See* 5 C.F.R. § 550.161(f); *see also* OPM

MEMORANDUM FOR DIRECTORS OF PERSONNEL (CPM 97-5) "Guidance on AUO Pay," June 13, 1997, Findings 2 & 3). However, the regulations provide certain limited exceptions for when ICE *may* choose to continue paying AUO to employees during periods when their duties would not otherwise qualify for AUO payment, namely:

a. During a **temporary assignment** to non-AUO duties for a period of not more than 10 consecutive workdays, and not more than 30 total workdays in a calendar year;

b. During **formally approved advanced training** directly related to AUO duties, for a period of not more than 60 workdays in a calendar year;

c. During a temporary assignment to non-AUO duties that is directly related to a **national emergency** declared by the President, for a period of not more than 30 consecutive workdays, and not more than 90 workdays in a calendar year;

d. During a period **following a job-related injury** where the employee is receiving continuation of pay under the Federal Employees' Compensation Act (FECA), 5 U.S.C. § 8101, *et seq.*, and the employee elects and is approved to take paid leave in lieu of FECA benefits, or if the employee is in receipt of FECA benefits and is in leave without pay status (where no payment would be made but authorization is continued to avoid reduction of retirement benefits). In these circumstances, AUO pay *must* be continued except where ICE has discontinued premium pay for the general position (as opposed to an individual position) which the employee occupies.

Computation of AUO Rate:

1. AUO is paid at rates of 10, 15, 20 and 25 percent of an employee's rate of basic pay, corresponding with the requirements to work three to five hours (10%), more than five hours to seven hours (15%), more than seven

hours to nine hours (20%), and more than nine hours (25%) of *"irregular or occasional"* overtime hours each week.

2. When computing the rate, ICE must:

   a. consider the available records of the hours of irregular or occasional overtime work that have been required of the specific employee in the past;

   b. consider other information bearing on the number of hours of duty that may reasonably be expected to be required of the employee in the future; and

   c. not consider the period of time under which an employee continues to receive premium pay pursuant to paragraphs (3)(a)(b) and (c) above in computing the average hours of irregular and occasional overtime.

Payment of AUO:

1. Although not all *"irregular or occasional"* overtime work serves to qualify an employee for the AUO premium, pursuant to 5 CFR § 550.163(b), once an employee is AUO certified, all overtime that was not regularly scheduled for an employee, and is thus *"irregular or occasional,"* is compensated through the AUO premium, as opposed to traditional FEPA overtime.

2. The only exception to the rule in Paragraph 1 is when the scheduling supervisor knew or should have known, in advance of the administrative workweek, that the specific employee was going to be needed to work overtime on the days and hours in question. (*See* 5 CFR § 610.121(b).) In those cases, the *"irregular"* overtime is treated as if it had been regularly scheduled, which for an AUO certified employee would result in the hours at issue being paid as FEPA overtime rather than through the AUO premium.

Interaction with other Payments:

1. AUO certified employees who are covered by the Fair

Labor Standards Act (FLSA), 29 U.S.C. § 201, *et seq.*, may receive a supplemental payment under the FLSA. The AUO premium is considered to constitute the "straight time" payment for each hour of irregular overtime and is supplemented by an additional "half time" payment for each hour of work that exceeds the applicable FLSA threshold. (*See* 5 CFR § 551.512(b); *Alexander v. US*, 1 Cl. Ct. 653 (1983); *Adams v. US*, 48 Fed.Cl. 602 (2001).)

2. AUO pay is subject to the same cumulative limitations that cover traditional FEPA overtime, including the biweekly pay limitation and the appropriations overtime cap.

3. Because the AUO premium is the exclusive method of payment for "*irregular or occasional*" overtime for AUO certified employees, those employees cannot receive compensatory time off (CTO) or any other payment under FEPA for those "*irregular or occasional*" hours of work.

4. Employees receiving AUO are also eligible for regularly scheduled overtime, Night Differential, Sunday Pay, and Holiday Pay, but may not claim AUO for those same hours. As noted above, hours that are compensable through AUO are not compensable with any other premium payment under FEPA.

APPENDIX C: ICE PREMIUM PAY GUIDE: FLSA

Introduction:

In 1938, the Fair Labor Standards Act (FLSA), 29 U.S.C. § 201, *et seq.*, was signed into law. In 1974, the FLSA was extended to employees of the United States Federal Government. *See* 1974 P.L. 93-259, 88 Stat. 55. Subsequently, the Federal Employees Pay Comparability Act of 1990 (FEPCA) was passed in an attempt to harmonize compensation under FEPA and the FLSA for employees covered by both statutes. *See* 1990 P.L.101-509 § 529, 104 Stat. 1389. The goal of the FLSA is to provide minimum standards for wages and overtime entitlements for time that is considered compensable hours of work. The primary principle is that employee time is compensable "hours of work" if (1) it is spent for the benefit of an agency; and (2) the employee's activities are controlled by the agency.

This section of the Guide is directed towards employees who are covered by the provisions of the FLSA ("FLSA nonexempt"). This Guide will not address issues related to determining what positions are or are not exempt from the provisions of the FLSA.

Statutory & Regulatory Authorities:

29 U.S.C. §§ 201-209; 5 CFR Part 551, Sections 101-104, 401-432, 501-541.

Rules:

1. At ICE, FLSA only applies to FLSA-nonexempt law enforcement officers **who are certified to receive AUO premium pay**.

2. An FLSA nonexempt employee is entitled to be paid "FLSA time and half" for each hour of overtime worked in excess of the appropriate FLSA threshold. The threshold for ICE law enforcement officers is eighty-five and a half (85.5) work hours per biweekly pay period. Work hours in excess of these thresholds are compensable with FLSA overtime.

3. For non-law enforcement/non-AUO employees on Compressed Work Schedules (CWS), the daily FLSA overtime threshold is based on hours of work in excess of the regularly scheduled work hours specific to the schedule, for example ten (10) hours for a "4-10" schedule. Similarly, for part-time employees, overtime hours are hours in excess of both 8 hours in a day and their scheduled hours for the day (including where the regular hours in the part-time schedule are compressed and greater than 8 in a day), and, on a weekly basis, over 40 hours.

FLSA Rate:

4. "FLSA time and a half" overtime is calculated differently for non-law enforcement employees and law enforcement employees, **because law enforcement employees are compensated with the AUO premium**. For non-law enforcement employees, FLSA overtime is compensated with the straight time rate of pay for all overtime hours worked, plus one-half the hourly regular rate of pay for all overtime hours worked. **For law enforcement employees**, FLSA overtime is compensated with the straight time rate of all regular overtime hours worked, the AUO premium for all hours of irregular overtime, and payment of an additional one-half the hourly regular rate of pay for all overtime hours over the applicable threshold, regular or irregular.

FLSA Hours of Work:

5. **The FLSA considers all hours that are compensable as hours of work under FEPA as compensable hours of work under the FLSA**. Such hours include time where an employee is required to be on duty, waiting or idle time that occurs during scheduled duty time, time in a

paid leave status, and travel time that is compensable under FEPA. (*See* 5 CFR § 551.401.) Unpaid non-duty status, such as leave without pay and furloughed time, is not compensable under the FLSA. This overlap includes identical definitions of what constitutes "standby" time as opposed to "on-call" time.

6. Unlike FEPA overtime, the FLSA does not concern itself with whether overtime is ordered or approved. Instead, **it is primarily concerned with whether an employee works for the benefit of an agency and at its direction and control.** Included in this concept is work that is *"suffered or permitted"* by an agency, where the agency knows or should know that an employee is engaged in work for its benefit and does not take action to disallow that work. Work that is *"suffered or permitted"* is compensable under the FLSA as hours of work.

   a. *Suffered or permitted"* work is, by definition, "irregular or occasional" overtime. For AUO certified employees, it is compensated through the AUO premium along with the corresponding supplemental FLSA payment, as described in Section 2.

7. The FLSA does not generally consider unscheduled work activities requiring ten minutes or less to perform to be compensable work hours; such activities are *"de minimis."* Note: this does not apply to ordered and approved overtime or on-call duties under FEPA.

8. Greater than *"de minimis"* time spent in preparatory or concluding activities that are closely related to and indispensable to the performance of an employee's primary duties are compensable as hours of work. Such activities should be regularly scheduled. Note: Notwithstanding Section 7 above, FEPA treats preparatory and concluding activities in the same way as the FLSA.

9. If an agency schedules a break period for meals, that time is a "bona fide" meal period, and not considered hours of work under the FLSA, as long as adequate

facilities exist to allow the employee to get away from his or her work and the break is largely uninterrupted. For FLSA ICE law enforcement employees, an agency must compensate any scheduled meal period where, notwithstanding having been temporarily relieved from duty, the employee returns to duty pursuant to his or her discretion under AUO. This time is compensated under AUO.

10.   FLSA compensates certain hours of travel that are not compensable under FEPA.

11.   The FLSA compensates time spent in training, as well as in preparation for training, if:

a. The training occurs during regularly scheduled working hours (including regularly scheduled overtime, noting that agencies should attempt to avoid scheduling training to occur during overtime hours);

b. The training occurs outside of regular working hours, where:

    i. the purpose of the training is to improve the employee's performance in his or her current position, including remedial or refresher training or training to learn a new process, technique or technology of the employee's current position (as opposed to "upward mobility" training or other courses designed to provide skills beyond those necessary in the current position, which is not compensable under the FLSA); **and**

    ii. the employee has been directed by Management to take the training, in that the employee's performance or continued retention in his or her position would be adversely affected by non-enrollment in the training course;

c. It is entry-level training, or other similar training,

which occurs outside of regularly scheduled working hours but is (1) given when the employee is already receiving premium pay for overtime, night, holiday, or Sunday work, (2) given at night because it concerns situations the employee must learn to handle at night, or (3) given on overtime, on a holiday or on a Sunday because ICE has determined that such scheduling is permissible, because the costs, including premium pay, are less than when the same training is confined only to regular duty hours.

12.　　　　The compensability of travel to and from training is governed by the same rules that govern all other forms of official travel.

13.　　　　The FLSA compensates time spent by an employee who has been directed to attend a lecture or conference if:

a. The lecture or conference occurs during regularly scheduled working hours; or

b. The lecture or conference occurs outside of regular working hours, but (1) the employee's attendance is directed by the agency, or (2) the employee performs compensable work for the agency during attendance.

14.　　　　If a FLSA qualified non-law enforcement employee is assigned to a shift of 24 or more consecutive hours of work, or a FLSA qualified law enforcement employee is assigned to a shift of greater than 24 consecutive hours of work, an agency may schedule up to eight (8) hours of *bona fide* break time for purposes of sleep, and deduct those hours from compensable time, so long as there are adequate facilities where an employee could generally enjoy uninterrupted sleep, and the sleep period extends for at least five hours. If the sleep period is interrupted by a call to duty, the time spent on duty is hours of work and cannot be deducted. If the sleep period does not extend for at least five consecutive hours, or there are not adequate facilities for sleep, the time is not deductible.

15.   FLSA overtime at ICE is also subject to the appropriations overtime cap limiting all forms of overtime compensation. ICE shall provide updates on earnings and the overtime cap.

APPENDIX D: ICE PREMIUM PAY GUIDE: LEAP

Introduction:

LEAP is a premium pay system designed to address the challenges of the substantial hours of *"unscheduled"* duty that are typically required of positions classified as *Criminal Investigators*, as defined by Congress and the Office of Personnel Management. Individuals in positions classified as

GS-1811 are eligible for LEAP.

The LEAP premium is fixed at 25% of the rate of basic pay. It compensates all hours of overtime work that meet the definition of *"Unscheduled Duty Hours,"* which includes all hours of *"irregular or occasional overtime"* as well as the first two hours of regularly scheduled overtime work on any day containing part of the criminal investigator's basic 40-hour workweek. Other hours of overtime continue to be paid under the provisions of Title 5/FEPA, but LEAP employees are exempt from the FLSA.

With a very narrow exception, all employees in *Criminal Investigator* positions are covered by LEAP beginning on the date of their entrance on duty, potentially including periods of basic training. However, LEAP may only be paid to employees certified to average two or more hours of *"unscheduled duty"* per regular workday. If an employee does not meet this *"substantial hours"* requirement, an Agency may suspend LEAP for the employee but must follow adverse action procedures. Agencies may also approve requests to temporarily "opt-out" of LEAP due to certain hardships on the understating that LEAP will not be paid and overtime generally not assigned during that period.

Statutory & Regulatory Authorities:
5 U.S.C. §§ 5542 & 5545a; 5 CFR Part 550, Sections 101-107, 181-187.

Rules:

1. The management of LEAP involves four sub-topics:

    a. Positions covered by LEAP;

    b. *Certification* for LEAP;

    c. *Suspension* of LEAP *certifications*; and
    d. Hours of work that qualify for *payment* of LEAP, as opposed to other forms of pay.

Positions Covered by LEAP.

2. LEAP is authorized only for positions that meet the definition of *Criminal Investigator*, set forth in 5 U.S.C. § 5545a(a)(2) and 5 C.F.R. §§ 550.103 and 550.181. Individuals in positions properly classified as GS-1811 are eligible for LEAP.

3. With a narrow exception that is inapplicable to ICE, all positions meeting the definitions of *Criminal Investigator* are covered by the provisions of LEAP.

Certification for LEAP.

4. Although the vast majority of criminal investigators are subject to the availability pay provisions, LEAP may be paid only to positions whose minimum annual average number of hours of "*unscheduled duty*" per regular workday is 2 hours or more, where the requirement for substantial hours is appropriately *certified* on an annual basis.

5. To the maximum extent feasible and consistent with ICE's law enforcement requirements, a substantial number of the hours needed to meet the minimum annual average of 2 hours or more per regular workday will be unscheduled duty hours actually worked.

6. *"Unscheduled duty"* under LEAP is defined as the hours during which a criminal investigator performs work or is in *"availability status"* that are not:

   a. Part of the employee's basic 40-hour workweek; or

   b. Overtime hours that were *"regularly scheduled"* in advance of the administrative workweek and compensated through traditional overtime payments under Title 5, including overtime hours in excess of ten (10) hours on a regular workday, or regularly scheduled hours of overtime work that occur on a scheduled day off.

7. In addition to Agency directed placement in availability status and order to perform irregular overtime, which is compensated through LEAP, *Criminal Investigators* may also "self-initiate" hours of irregular or occasional overtime work or availability status, without specific supervisory pre-approval, based upon the investigators' determination that the work or availability status is necessary to meet the needs of Agency, subject to Agency policy and a requirement for after-the- fact approval. .

   a. If the "self-initiated" hours of work or availability status are subsequently approved and consistent with Agency policy, these hours qualify as *"unscheduled duty"* for purposes of LEAP. At ICE, self-initiation of unscheduled duty should only occur in extraordinary circumstances.

   b. If the "self-initiated" hours of work or availability status are not case- or operation- specific, or if they occur on a non-workday but do not involve the actual performance of work, they should not be approved, and will not qualify as *"unscheduled duty"* for purposes of LEAP.

   c. Hours that would not constitute hours of work under FEPA or time in "on-call" status will not qualify as "unscheduled duty" for purposes of LEAP, including:

      i.   Time spent commuting from home to a criminal investigator's duty station on a regular workday and vice versa via a government-owned vehicle (GOV) or a privately-owned vehicle (POV);

ii. Travel time outside the duty station or temporary work location during non-duty hours that does not meet the compensable overtime criteria in 5 U.S.C. § 5542 (b)(2)(B) and 5 CFR 550.1 12(g); or

iii. Time spent in training that is covered by the premium pay prohibition of 5 CFR 410.402.

8. To determine whether a criminal investigator is meeting the *"substantial hours"* requirement of a minimum of two hours of *"unscheduled duty"* per regular workday, an Agency divides the total number of *"unscheduled duty"* hours for the annual period by the number of *"regular workdays"* in the certification period, as explained more fully in subsections 8(a) and (b), below:

a. The total number of *"unscheduled duty"* hours counted towards this requirement include only *"unscheduled duty"* hours on a regular workday and hours *where work is actually performed* (as opposed to where an employee is available) during *"unscheduled duty"* hours on days that are not regular workdays.

b. The number of *"regular workdays"* is the total number of days in a criminal investigator's basic workweek where at least four hours of work are performed. The four hour minimum does not include: (1) overtime hours, (2) unscheduled duty hours compensated via LEAP, (3) hours spent in Agency approved training, (4) hours of official travel where the travel time is not compensable as hours of work under Title 5/FEPA, (5) hours spent on approved leave or other excused absence with pay, (6) periods of leave without pay (LWOP) and LWOP compensated in compliance with the Federal Employees Compensation Act (FECA), commonly referred to as Office of Workers Compensation Programs (OWCP), (7) periods of suspension for disciplinary reasons when an employee is in a non-pay status, or (8) periods in a part-time status, where an employee is decertified from LEAP.

9. In order to initiate LEAP, a newly-hired *Criminal Investigator* and his or her appropriate supervisor must make an initial certification to the head of the Agency (or designee) that the criminal investigator is expected to meet the *"substantial hours"* requirement during the upcoming 1-year period. This is a prerequisite to receiving LEAP, and there are no provisions for a waiver of this requirement.

10. In order to continue LEAP, each *Criminal Investigator* who is not suspended from LEAP, along with the appropriate supervisor, must make an annual recertification to the head of the Agency (or designee) that the criminal investigator currently meets and is expected to continue meeting the *"substantial hours"* requirement. At ICE, this recertification is made electronically, by January 31 of each calendar year, and covers from the preceding January 1 through December 31.

Voluntary and Involuntary Suspensions of LEAP Certification.

11. Once a criminal investigator is certified for LEAP, it is incumbent on the employee and management to monitor the performance of unscheduled duty to determine whether the *"substantial hours"* requirement is being met.

12. If management determines that an investigator who is certified for LEAP is not meeting or will not meet the *"substantial hours"* requirement, management may act to deny or cancel a certification and suspend LEAP payment. This may be based on a finding that the investigator failed to perform unscheduled duty (assigned or reported overtime work or designated availability hours), in sufficient quantities or at all, or will not be able to perform unscheduled duty for an extended period of time due to physical or health reasons.

13. An involuntary suspension of LEAP resulting

from the denial or cancellation of certification, such as described above, constitutes a reduction of pay under 5 U.S.C. § 7512 and thus must be initiated under the adverse actions procedures set forth in 5 C.F.R. part 752. If the certification was valid at the time it was made, the suspension will be prospective. Guidance on adverse actions is available from the Office of Human Capital, Employee and Labor Relations.

14.   In addition to involuntary suspensions, LEAP may also be suspended voluntarily at an employee's request and with management agreement. A criminal investigator may make a written request that he or she be generally assigned no overtime work, including unscheduled duty, and a corresponding suspension of LEAP, based upon personal or family hardships or other circumstances that would preclude him or her meeting the substantial hours requirement. The criminal investigator must sign and date the Law Enforcement Availability Pay Waiver, indicating the understanding that LEAP will be voluntarily suspended, and thus not paid, during the designated period. Managers and supervisors will consider such requests for relief for a specific period of time on a case-by-case basis.

15.   If the request is approved, the supervisor does not need to initiate adverse action procedures, but must initiate a personnel action to stop the payment of LEAP. If the request is denied, the criminal investigator shall continue to perform the full range of the duties of his or her position. At ICE, however, if a request to temporarily "opt-out" of LEAP is denied, the criminal investigator may appeal that denial to the Executive Associate Director of his or her Directorate or the Assistant Director of his or her Program Office. A criminal investigator may continue to receive LEAP during periods of approved leave.

16.   If the period of an approved voluntary suspension of LEAP appears to be insufficient, a criminal investigator may request an extension of the voluntary suspension, in writing, under the same

procedures described above. Such requests will be considered by management on a case-by-case basis and a denial may be appealed in the same manner as the initial request.

17.   A criminal investigator who is suspended from LEAP, whether voluntarily or involuntarily, must be recertified at the end of the period of suspension of LEAP, and a personnel action must be initiated so that the payment of LEAP may resume.

Payment of LEAP:

18.   A criminal investigator will be paid LEAP equal to 25 percent of his or her rate of basic pay, as defined in 5 CFR § 550.103. LEAP is paid only during periods when a criminal investigator is receiving basic pay.

19.   In certain circumstances, LEAP continues to be paid when no *"unscheduled duty"* is performed on the workday, and the lack of such work hours is not factored into the calculation of a criminal investigator's average daily performance of *"unscheduled duty"* to meet the *"substantial hours"* requirement. These circumstances include:

a. Days of excused paid absences, such as holidays and annual, sick, administrative, military, funeral, or court leave;

b. Days of officially approved training; or

c. Days spent performing officially approved travel that does not constitute hours of work, such as travel for relocation purposes.

20.   LEAP is subject to the biweekly premium pay limitation prescribed by 5 U.S.C. § 5547(c) and any annual overtime limitation prescribed by the annual Appropriations Act.

21.   LEAP will not be paid to a criminal investigator in part-time status, since LEAP is premium pay for unscheduled duty in excess of a 40-hour workweek.

Interaction with other Payments:

22.   LEAP is the exclusive premium payment for all "unscheduled duty hours." However, a criminal investigator receiving LEAP may also receive, when appropriate and officially ordered or approved:

a. Regularly scheduled overtime under 5 U.S.C. § 5542(a) that occurs on a scheduled day off, or that is in excess of 10 hours of work on a day during the basic 40-hour workweek (regardless of whether the ten hours were scheduled or unscheduled) which is compensated under the generally applicable provisions of Title 5/FEPA;

b. Night Pay under 5 U.S.C. § 5545(a) for qualifying hours that do not constitute "unscheduled duty hours;"

c. Sunday Pay under 5 U.S.C. § 5546(a) for qualifying hours that do not constitute "unscheduled duty hours;"

d. Holiday Pay under 5 U.S.C. § 5546(d) for qualifying hours that do not constitute "unscheduled duty hours;" and

e. Compensatory Time Off for Travel, when the hours of travel are not compensable as *"unscheduled duty"* hours under LEAP, including designated *"availability hours."*

23.   Criminal investigators receiving LEAP are not entitled to receive:

a. Overtime pay under the FLSA, as they are FLSA exempt (not covered by the FLSA);

b. Regularly scheduled standby duty pay under 5 U.S.C. § 5545(c)(I);

c. Administratively Uncontrollable Overtime;

d. Compensatory Time Off (CTO) in lieu of pay for irregular or occasional overtime work;

e. Hazardous duty pay under 5 U.S.C. § 5545(d) for unscheduled duty hours credited to LEAP .

24.   LEAP is treated as basic pay for:

a. Advances in pay under 5 U.S.C. § 5524a;

b. Severance pay under 5 U.S.C. § 5595(c);

c. Workers' compensation under 5 U.S.C. § 8114(e);

d. Retirement benefits under 5 U.S.C. § 8331(3) and 5 U.S.C. § 8401 (4);

e. Thrift Savings Plan under 5 U.S.C. §§ 8431-8440f; and

f. Life insurance under 5 U.S.C. § 8704(c).

25.   LEAP is not treated as basic pay when calculating the cost-of-living allowances or other allowances and differentials. LEAP is also not treated as basic pay when calculating retirement benefits under 5 U.S.C. § 8331(3) and 5 U.S.C. § 8401(4) for non-foreign areas outside the 50 States and the District of Columbia (e.g., the Commonwealth of Puerto Rico, the U.S. Virgin Islands, Guam, the Northern Mariana Islands, etc.).

---

[1] In 1997, a federal district court in California approved the Flores Settlement Agreement (*Flores*) after over a decade of litigation. The underlying lawsuit, a class action filed on behalf of immigrant children against the legacy Immigration and Naturalization Service (INS), challenged the conditions of immigrant children in U.S. government custody.

Flores sets forth foundational principles and critical protections regarding the care, custody, and release of immigrant children who are in federal custody. Initially, *Flores* applied only to the INS, but, with its dissolution, the requirements of *Flores* presently extend to the Department of Homeland Security (DHS) (which oversees care for accompanied children) and the Department of Health and Human Services' (HHS) Office of Refugee Resettlement (ORR) (which oversees care for unaccompanied children).

[2] February 9, 2017 Presidential Executive Order on Enforcing Federal Law with Respect to Transnational Criminal Organizations and Preventing International Trafficking.

[3] Best Places to Work employee engagement score, calculated by the Partnership for Public Service and Boston Consulting Group, ranked ICE 348 out of 420 federal government agencies regarding employee morale. They used three different questions in the U.S. OPM's Federal Employee Viewpoint Survey to calculate the ranking. The questions used were: "I recommend my organization as a good place to work. Considering everything, how satisfied are you with your job? Considering everything, how satisfied are you with your organization?"

[4] Another option is to discontinue ERO and place its resources and responsibilities beyond 100 miles of the Southern border under HSI. This option will require additional monies due to the required specialized training that the officers will need to convert to Special Agents, and then to receive the GS-1811-13 grade.

[5] Congressional Research Service (Federal Land Ownership: Overview and Data), February 21, 2020, reported that "The federal government owns roughly 640 million acres, about 28% of the 2.27 billion acres of land in the United States. Four major federal land management agencies administer 606.5 million acres of this land (as of September 30, 2018). They are the Bureau of Land Management (BLM), Fish and Wildlife Service (FWS), and National Park Service (NPS) in the Department of the Interior (DOI) and the Forest Service (FS) in the Department of Agriculture. A fifth agency, the Department of Defense (excluding the U.S. Army Corps of Engineers), administers 8.8 million acres in the United States (as of September 30, 2017), consisting of military bases, training ranges, and more. Together, the five agencies manage about 615.3 million acres, or 27% of the U.S. land base. Many other agencies administer the remaining federal acreage."

[6] Noted on an October 2014 GAO report to Congress regarding Immigration Detention.

[7] This program makes and implements placement decisions in the best interests of UAC to ensure that they are in the least restrictive setting possible while in federal custody. The majority of UAC are cared for through a network of state licensed ORR-funded care providers, which provide classroom education, mental and medical health services, case management, and socialization/recreation. ORR/DCS funds programs to provide a continuum of care for children, including foster care, group homes, and residential treatment centers. The division also coordinates a legal access project assuring that these children have information about their legal rights and receive an individual legal screening to assess their chances of legal relief. Finally, ORR/DCS provides family reunification services to facilitate safe and timely placement with family members or other qualified sponsors.

[8] In 1997, a federal district court in California approved the Flores Settlement Agreement (*Flores*) after over a decade of litigation. The underlying lawsuit, a class action filed on behalf of immigrant children against the legacy Immigration and Naturalization Service (INS), challenged the conditions of immigrant children in U.S. government custody.

Flores sets forth foundational principles and critical protections regarding the care, custody, and release of immigrant children who are in federal custody. Initially, *Flores* applied only to the INS, but, with its dissolution, the requirements of *Flores* presently extend to the Department of Homeland Security (DHS) (which oversees care for accompanied children) and the Department of Health and Human Services' (HHS) Office of Refugee Resettlement (ORR) (which oversees care for unaccompanied children).

[9] I-830 (Alien Address Notification to the Department of Justice) – The Form I-830 form is. used to notify the DOJ Executive Office for Immigration Review (EOIR) of changes to. the alien's address.

[10] December 2016 - Mortality in State Prisons, 2001-2014 - Statistical Tables -Margaret E. Noonan, *BJS Statistician: Found between 2001 and 2014, there were 50,785 prisoner deaths in state and federal prisons. The majority (45,640) of prisoner deaths occurred in state prisons. The state prisoner average annual mortality rate (256 per 100,000 state prisoners) was 14% higher than the federal prisoner mortality rate (225 per 100,000 federal prisoners) between 2001 and 2014.*

[11] Acting ICE Director Tom Homan provided these statistics during his testimony before Congress.

[12] FRCs are intended to detain unlawfully present immigrant families while they are going through their immigration proceedings, awaiting to be removed from the United States or their release from custody.

[13] Wikipedia - The United States Census of 1940, conducted by the Census Bureau, determined the resident population of the United States to be 132,164,569.

[14] Wikipedia - From 1941 to 1950, 1,035,000 people immigrated to the U.S., including 226,000 from Germany, 139,000 from the UK, 171,000 from Canada, 60,000 from Mexico and 57,000 from Italy. The Displaced Persons Act of 1948 finally allowed the displaced people of World War II to start immigrating.

[15] Generally, workers in the United States in H-2B status who extend their stay, change employers, or change the terms and conditions of employment will not be subject to the cap. Similarly, H-2B workers who have previously been counted against the cap in the same fiscal year that the proposed employment begins will not be subject to the cap if the employer names them on the petition and indicates that they have already been counted. The spouse and children of H-2B workers classified as H-4 nonimmigrants also do not count against this cap. Additionally, petitions for the following types of workers are exempt from the H-2B cap:
- Fish roe processors, fish roe technicians or supervisors of fish roe processing;
- Workers performing labor or services in the Commonwealth of Northern Mariana Islands or Guam from No. 28, 2009, until Dec. 31, 2029.

Once the H-2B cap is reached, USCIS may only accept petitions for H-2B workers who are exempt or not subject to the H-2B cap.

[16] Calculation based on an unlawfully present population of 10 million times .67 (Mexico and Central American unlawful population) times .67 (percentage in the labor force) times one thousand (amount of fine)

[17] In general, prosecutorial discretion is the authority that an agency or officer has to decide what, if any, charges to bring against a party and how to pursue each case. In other words, it means that an agency can choose whether or not to file charges. In the immigration law context, prosecutorial discretion refers to the Immigration and Customs Enforcement (ICE) office and the power they have to discontinue working on a deportation case. If the office declines to pursue a case, then it means that the office has favorably exercised prosecutorial discretion.

[18] According to the United States Citizenship and Immigration Services (USCIS), deferred action is defined as "a discretionary determination to defer a deportation of an individual as

MR JOE MICHAEL SIFUENTEZ

an act of prosecutorial discretion."

[19] A **stay of deportation** is an order directly the Department of Homeland Security to refrain from removing an immigrant from the United States. It can be granted from the Board of Immigration Appeals (BIA) or from a Federal Court. In the alternative, an alien can apply with ICE for an administrative I-246 stay of removal.

[20] Worksite enforcement is one aspect of overall immigration enforcement, focused on identifying the workers who are not authorized to work as well as the employers who knowingly hire unauthorized workers.

[21] An official statement of a complaint over something believed to be wrong or unfair.

[22] Arbitration is a private process where disputing parties agree that one or several individuals can make a decision about the dispute after receiving evidence and hearing arguments. Arbitration is different from mediation because the neutral arbitrator has the authority to make a decision about the dispute.

[23] The **Merit Systems Protection Board** (**MSPB**) is an independent quasi-judicial agency established in 1979 to protect federal **merit systems** against partisan political and other prohibited personnel practices and to ensure adequate **protection** for federal employees against abuses by agency management.